YOU'RE NOT CRAZY – IT'S YOUR MOTHER

Please note that the stories of women shared here are either reprinted by permission, or are composite sample stories.

If you find *You're Not Crazy* to be valuable, please do spread the word so others can have the confidence to buy it. Online reviews are the best way to commend it – on websites of the most popular booksellers, and through your own networks if you use social media or a blog. Thank you!

YOU'RE NOT CRAZY – IT'S YOUR MOTHER

Understanding and healing for
daughters of narcissistic mothers

DANU MORRIGAN

DARTON·LONGMAN + TODD

You are not broken and in need of fixing.
You are wounded and in need of healing.

First published in 2012 by
Darton, Longman and Todd Ltd
1 Spencer Court
140 – 142 Wandsworth High Street
London SW18 4JJ

Reprinted 2013, 2015

ISBN: 978-0-232-52929-6

Designed by Judy Linard
Printed and bound by Bell & Bain, Glasgow

This book is dedicated to 'Light' who has been my mentor, ally, friend, soul-sister, challenger, colleague and wonderful fun on this amazing journey.

To Maggie, my dearest friend and soul-sister, who has supported me in every way and been my rock.

To David, my son, who helped me heal as I discovered, through parenting him, what a healthy parent-child relationship could be. And who is just all-round awesome.

To all the DONMs who have made the forum the wonderful place it is, filled with the vibrant energy of healing, of tears, of laughter, of support, of strength and determination.

And above all, to all the DONMs who did not survive being raised by a narcissist.

CONTENTS

INTRODUCTION

If you were drawn to the title of this book, then I suspect that the information here is exactly what you need.

The fact is that it's more than possible that you are *not* as crazy as you always felt, but rather that it's *your mother* causing all the upset and angst and confusion and doubt that you live with throughout your life.

And it's possible that she is doing that because she has something called Narcissistic Personality Disorder, or NPD.

In a nutshell, people with NPD have an overblown opinion of themselves. They consider that they are perfect, and (crucially) have an absolute need to *continue* thinking of themselves as perfect. They also have an insatiable need for attention from others. They have no empathy for anyone else as a real person, seeing other people only as a source of the attention they crave.

Being raised by a narcissist is a special kind of crazy. It is a pure and laser-sharp form of psychological and emotional abuse. But even more devastatingly, it is an invisible abuse. Neither the perpetrator nor the victim even knows it's happening. The perpetrator (the narcissist) doesn't think she's abusing anyone because, by definition, she's perfect, remember, and perfect people don't do imperfect things like abuse people. And the abuse victim, the daughter – this would be *you* – doesn't realise she's abused because she believes her mother's lies and thinks that everything is her fault, that she is the one who is broken.

And so, there are two layers of abuse and dysfunction going on. There's the first layer, which is the original bad treatment, about which we will talk a lot more. And there's the second layer, which is the denial that the bad treatment ever happened! And that's the bit that leads to you thinking that it's you that's crazy, and hence the title of this book. (Actually, there's a third layer too, which we explore later.)

So, who am I and why am I writing this book?

My name is Danu Morrigan and I believe I am the daughter of a narcissistic mother. I don't know, of course. She was never professionally diagnosed, and it is only my totally unprofessional best guess to explain the crazy that I experienced. But it fits together like a jigsaw puzzle.

I always had a difficult relationship with my mother. There were good times for sure, but I could never relax even then, because I was only ever one wrong word or expressed opinion away from her disapproval, her snapped, 'That's enough, Danu!', and me being put back in my box.

I used to think of it as her pulling rank – that she always held the power in the relationship and we could be friends all right, but only ever on her terms and as long as I remembered my place, which was subordinate to her. It was like walking through a beautiful flower-strewn meadow, but the path was on a cliff-top and one wrong step would send me plummeting. The eternal vigilance meant I could never relax.

I just accepted this, though. You do, don't you? It's your mother after all. I just endured as best as I could. My husband was used to me ranting in upset and hurt after every visit, but neither of us questioned why I was putting me (and him, and my son) through this agony. I did often wish I could just cut off contact with her and my father (more about fathers later), realising that if they were friends rather than family I would have done that years ago. But again, you can't, can you, not when it's your family? (Hint – yes, you can! I realise that now and am going to share this information with you. I wish I had known this *decades* ago.)

This was the situation until September of 2008. I was usually pretty adroit at keeping my friends, and anyone else I respected, well away from my parents, but on this occasion my dear friend Maggie came to lunch with them.

It was fairly standard stuff: my mother talked non-stop at us; no one else got a look in. She and my father had just come back from holiday and she talked non-stop about that. We were at the restaurant for 2 hours and 25 minutes exactly, and apart from ordering food and such essential conversation, she spoke on and on. And on. No detail was too obscure to exclude.

It was funny nearly. I took pity on my then-12-year-old son, who was just languishing totally ignored, and whispered that he could go out to the car and read his book. He disappeared with an enthusiasm that would have been funny if it wasn't so sad. Neither my mother nor father acknowledged, nor even seemed to register, his disappearance.

Then Maggie had had enough, and excused herself and left, ostensibly for a cigarette but really (I guessed and she later confirmed) because she could not bear it any more. My mother did acknowledge her disappearance with a sneering comment about smokers, but that was it.

All these lunch guests disappearing, like a murder mystery, and it didn't faze my mother at all; she just kept talking, going on and on like the Duracell Bunny.

Afterwards Maggie was full of a combination of shock and apologies. Shock at how bad it had been, and apologies that she hadn't realised before. She acknowledged that I had told her that my parents were difficult, but she had had no idea how bad it was.

She pointed out elements about the encounter that I hadn't really noticed, accustomed as I was to this treatment. Such as the fact that neither of my parents even spoke to my son. Not once, after the initial hellos. They totally ignored him. And this was effectively their only grandchild. (They were already estranged from my two siblings who are the parents of the other grandchildren and to my knowledge have never met them.) They ignored my sister who was there, too. And neither of them had had the manners to speak to Maggie at all, despite not knowing her. She didn't mind for her own sake, she said, but it just was so rude.

It was a revelation for me. An epiphany. You mean this was *objectively* bad? I knew I didn't enjoy it, but it was bad by any standard?

In that moment I just knew I didn't want to see either of my parents ever again. I knew I wasn't going to. Maggie's perspective somehow gave me the permission I thought I needed, and that I had been craving for years.

(I am hoping that this book can do the same for *you*. Give you the permission you think you need. In truth, you, like me, do not need any permission to remove yourself from an abuser's clutches.)

But how would I tell my parents this? There would be *war*. All my life the simplest complaint or request for better treatment had ended very badly. Had ended, indeed, in me being royally abused, invalidated and gaslighted (of which more below).

All that for a mild complaint. All part, as I now know, of the unhealthy abusive, narcissistic dynamic. How much worse would they react to me cutting off contact? I was terrified. How would I broach the subject with them? Or did I have to? Maybe I could just not say anything. Just disappear on them. But that'd never work. Around and around went my thoughts.

Two weeks passed with me fretting over this, feeling physically nauseous and terrified the whole time.

And then my father rang. They had had such a good time at that lunch, he said, that they'd like to do it again. Would I be free that day?

Shaking I said that I would not meet them for lunch. 'Why?' he asked, in the low, dangerous tone which, all my life, terrified me.

'Because,' I said, 'the last time was an ordeal and I'm anxious not to repeat that.'

Why was it an ordeal, he asked, still in that dangerous tone.

Still shaking, my stomach heaving, my voice quavering, I told him what had been wrong with the day. I was careful to use 'I' words and state things calmly and talk about undesired actions rather than talk about them personally. But that was not enough to save me.

He took a slow, deep, shuddering breath during which I thought I'd have a heart attack, and then said what he always said if I dared complain about anything, 'Well, you think *you're* so perfect!'

There then followed an hour or so of abuse by first him and then by my mother as he handed over to her for the second shift. It was hell. They eviscerated everything about me, trying to shred and diminish me rather than sort anything out.

Eventually I got off the phone, nauseous and shaking, with nothing resolved.

Two weeks of silence passed, and then, out of the blue, the thought came to me, clearly and calmly: 'She has Narcissistic Personality Disorder.' I have no idea how that thought occurred – I wasn't even thinking of her at the time. And while I did know about NPD, having researched it for another project, I had not made the connection until that moment.

That epiphany started me on a long journey which has led to this book, and to sharing this information with you.

I now run a website and forum for daughters of narcissistic mothers (or DONMs as we call ourselves): www.daughtersofnarcissistic mothers.com. In the three years I have had this website and forum I have been privileged to hear of many DONMs' experiences – most of them a *lot* worse than mine; I realise now that my mother is mild on the spectrum, and yet the havoc even that caused was huge. I have therefore learned a lot about narcissistic mothers, narcissistic abuse, and the effects on DONMs, and this is what I am sharing with you now.

Please know that I have no professional qualifications in this line, and I do not claim any. What I am is a fellow-traveller, like you, a survivor of the invisible and horrendous abuse that is narcissism. But I am a traveller who has travelled far along this route, and spoken with many other journeyers, and who knows and understands what it is like. It is in this spirit that I share the rest of the information in this book with you.

The book discusses what Narcissistic Personality Disorder is, how it manifests in your mother, and the effects on you as her daughter. We then discuss what your options are regarding relating to her in future, and the impact of knowing the truth. And finally, and essentially, we discuss how to heal from this dysfunction. As part of the healing I share an amazing technique called EFT (Emotional Freedom Technique). I came across this about ten years ago when I was on my journey to fix all the things I thought were wrong with me. It involves tapping on acupuncture points and is so, so good at removing negative emotions and limiting beliefs. Much more about this in due course.

Part One
ALL ABOUT NARCISSISTIC PERSONALITY DISORDER

1
WHAT IS NARCISSISTIC PERSONALITY DISORDER?

The official definition of NPD is in Appendix I on page 190. But it is hard for laypeople to relate to, and is in the process of being amended anyway so might be out of date by the time you read this. And so I give you instead a layperson's guide to NPD, to help you recognise it.

Note also that there are 'cousin' personality disorders of NPD, and your mother might have some of these too as there can be overlap (hence the official criteria being amended). These 'cousins' are Borderline Personality Disorder, Histrionic Personality Disorder, and Anti-Social Personality Disorder (sociopathy). Do read up on these, and see the link to more information in Appendix II on page 191.

Here is my Layperson's Guide to Narcissists:

She is the centre of the universe and absolutely everything – *everything* – is therefore about her.

When I say that everything is about her, I mean it quite literally. I am not exaggerating, I am not using hyperbole. It is (for her) literally true. I know that it is difficult, verging on impossible, for normal people to get their heads around such breathtaking self-centredness, but the more you can begin to imagine it, the more you can get a glimpse of understanding of narcissism. I repeat: *everything* is about her. Her husband's death, your stillborn baby, a regional disaster: all important or relevant only in as much as they impact on her.

She has zero empathy.

She cannot (or will not) put herself in anyone else's shoes to feel how they feel. Again, normal people find it hard to imagine this, but this is the fact of it. Empathy is an intrinsic part of what makes us human (although in fairness, other animals have it too; it's not unique to us), and it is hard to imagine someone without it. But that is the situation with narcissists. No empathy, whatsoever, ever, no matter what's going on.

She needs to believe she is perfect and does no wrong, ever.

Again, this is not exaggeration. She believes she is quite literally perfect and does no wrong, ever. *By definition* she does no wrong. So if she did it, it's the right thing to do. Or if it is indisputably wrong, she cannot have done it, despite all evidence to the contrary.

Everyone has to acknowledge that she is both the centre of the universe and perfect, and treat her accordingly.

It's not enough for *her* to know that she's the Centre Of The Universe, and perfect, oh no. Everyone else has to know this too, or at least behave in a way that respects her position, and constantly reinforce this belief for her.

The main way she knows that someone is honouring her position as Centre Of The Universe is if they're paying her attention. Lots of attention. The kind of attention she prefers is admiration, but fear works well, too, if that's all she can get. And pity, failing even that.

This attention is called *Narcissistic Supply*. It's described as being like a drug for narcissists, but I think it's much more akin to food and drink, i.e. essential for their survival. (In this case, their psychic survival.) This is why they will do anything needed to ensure their Narcissistic Supply.

You, as her daughter, are in a very good place to give her this Narcissistic Supply. You're available, probably, and you've been trained to do that since birth. It's an endless job as her tanks need constant filling. She needs attention *constantly,* not occasionally or intermittently. Her tanks are more a sieve than a waterproof container.

Now most people like attention, don't get me wrong. (Having said that, daughters of narcissistic mothers can struggle with that, of which more below.) We can all feel stroked and pleased when people are focussed on us. But the difference is that we *like* it, we don't *need* it, as they do. And we don't desire it constantly, again, as they do.

In a very real sense, narcissists are stuck being emotionally between three and six years old. Children of that age go through an appropriately narcissistic stage, when everything is about them. Most of us grow out of it. Narcissists don't. So, by being raised by a narcissist you were raised with someone with the emotional maturity of a small child. No wonder it was so awful. It's equivalent to being raised by a toddler.

IGNORING MOTHERS AND ENGULFING MOTHERS

Narcissistic mothers fall into two categories: Ignoring Mother and Engulfing Mother.

The Ignoring Mother has zero interest in you. You will be mostly ignored, perhaps neglected. You will probably not be taught basic self-care techniques, for example. She won't come to your school events, or if she does (for the look of it, lest others think less of her for not going), she won't show much interest. She'll probably talk to you of how well another child did, with only perfunctory praise for you, if you get any praise at all.

This is hugely disconcerting as it means that you never feel seen. I myself had an Ignoring Mother, and grew up always to be the clown, the entertainer, always 'on'. Not in an ego way, not to be adored or admired. Merely to be seen, to know that I existed. It was exhausting, both for me and, I am certain, for those who experienced it. I now realise I do not have to do this any more and it is the biggest relief. I also think my life-long weight issues had to do with this – with taking up enough room in the world so that I knew I existed.

However, bad and all as it is to have an Ignoring Mother, in truth it's much worse having an Engulfing mother.

Engulfing Mothers think, as do all narcissists, that it's all about themselves. Unfortunately they seem to perceive 'themselves' as including their daughter. Their daughter is not a separate person for them, but merely an extension of themselves. And as such the Engulfing Mother will try to run the daughter's life for her. She'll have an opinion on everything from the clothes she wears to her family-planning decisions.

Geri, who has an Engulfing Mother, relates how her mother would even ask intimate questions about her and her husband's sex life! And she'd ask it as if it was the most natural thing in the world, and Geri was being *most* unreasonable not to want to share that information. Equally, an Engulfing Mother might share inappropriate information with you, such as details about *her* sex life, and she might start doing this even when you're very young.

The Engulfing Mother will not see any differences between you and her. She might insist that you like cabbage when in fact you hate it – but she loves it. Or, as happened to Amy on our forum, she might make you put on a jumper when she's cold, despite the fact that you're insisting that you're warm enough. She truly cannot see the difference between her and you. If she loves cabbage or is cold, then you *must* too.

They might also try to take over your children. Annie relates how her mother received news of her new baby's birth by telling people,

'My new baby was born today'. They might try and get the children to call them 'Mamma' and their own mother by her given name. They probably will undermine their daughter's parenting rules without scruple or concern. 'I know Mummy said you can't have sweets before dinner, but I'm telling you that you can. Don't mind what Mummy says.'

In this way the abuse continues to the next generation as this, of course, is totally confusing for the children.

Daughters of Engulfing Mothers can end up living near their mothers, and having their mothers involved in every aspect of their lives. On the surface this all looks wonderful – who doesn't appreciate a close mother-daughter relationship after all? The daughter herself might even think she has a great relationship with her mother and is so lucky. She might say, and mean it, 'My mother is my best friend'.

And so, it's far harder to extricate yourself from the clutches of an Engulfing Narcissist because you don't even realise you're trapped. And even when you do realise this, the psychological tentacles which are wrapped around you are very difficult to remove. In addition there can be practical and logistical tentacles too, such as living together in a co-owned house, which just add to the problem.

WHAT CAUSES NPD? CAN SHE HELP IT?

It has been known for years that Narcissistic Personality Disorder runs in families, but it was not known whether that was nature (i.e. genetic) or nurture (i.e. caused by abuse or over-indulgence). The consensus seemed to be more towards thinking it was caused by how the child was reared, but with no basis for that as there had been little research done on it.

On our forum we have long considered that there must be a genetic component because so many DONMs have narcissistic children, despite raising them well. And recently this has been borne out by a study (by W. J. Livesley, et al at the University of British Columbia) which has found a clear genetic link.

So that means she can't help it?

Yes and no. She can't help having NPD. But she can still help how she acts. NPD is not a defence in court. She is not insane. She chooses her actions. We discuss this more in due course.

2

HOW NARCISSISM MANIFESTS ITSELF IN YOUR MOTHER

The elements of narcissism shared above manifest in different ways in your mother's behaviour and her treatment of you. I am sure you will recognise many of them.

She is either glowing or huffing.

One of two possible situations applies to your narcissistic mother at any time: she is either getting enough Narcissistic Supply or she is not. There is no neutral ground for her. I coined the terms *Narcissistic Glow* and *Narcissistic Huff*, respectively, to describe the narcissistic mother's reaction to those two situations.

Narcissistic Glow is the glow and joy and incandescence, and quiver and excitement that narcissists get when their narcissistic egos are being fed. They can look truly beautiful and happy when they're experiencing the Narcissistic Glow. The Glow can also appear in satisfaction when they've upset you or otherwise gained supremacy over you. One DONM described her mother as being 'incredibly beautiful' when she had this glow.

The corollary to the Glow is the *Narcissistic Huff*. It describes the sulk, huff, glower, mood, pursed lips, etc they manifest when they're

NOT getting enough Narcissistic Supply. This is a danger sign, and often presages *Narcissistic Rage*, of which more below.

She re-writes history.

Because she is perfect all the time, she cannot do any wrong, by definition. Therefore if you bring any wrongdoing of hers to her attention, she will have a range of defences to make it not so. This is akin to the wishful thinking of a toddler who will *swear*, up down and sideways, that she did not eat the cake, regardless of the chocolate stains all over her face. She thinks that if she says it often enough and hard enough, it'll be true.

So your narcissistic mother is quite happy to rewrite history. This is known as *gaslighting*. It's named after a 1940s film called, appropriately, *Gaslight*, where the baddie husband turned down the gas supply in the attic, so that the gas lights in the house flickered due to insufficient fuel. When the wife commented on this, he laughed at her and told her she was imagining it, that the lights were perfect – and that was his first step to convincing her she was losing her mind.

The first line of gaslighting defence is to simply deny the incident even happened. You might say, 'Mum, it upset me when you said in front of everyone that I'd put on weight'. She will look you full in the eye and announce with absolute certainty, 'I never said that'.

And if she says it with enough conviction and certainty (oh, and she will!), then you'll very possibly end up believing her statement over your own perceptions and memories.

So, not only does she abuse you (telling you that you're fat in front of your friends, in this example), but then she denies it even happened! It's a double-whammy. So you're left reeling, feeling hurt about the first layer of abuse, and confused about the second. This leads you to doubt your own perception, to question your own sense of reality, and is, in my opinion, one of the two worst aspects of the abuse we daughters of narcissistic mothers (DONMs) receive.

(Teaching us that we're born broken, as explained on page 56, is the other.)

Consider too that as her daughter, you've been subject to this from the day of your birth, so you have had days and months and *years* of this psychological abuse. Add to that the fact that children are biologically programmed to believe their parents, and it makes it even crueller because we are so incredibly susceptible to the lies.

She might pooh-pooh your memory and say patronisingly, 'Oh no, dear, I didn't say that. Your hearing/memory is going, you'd want to check that out. What I said was that it was good that you *hadn't* put on weight'.

My own mother said once, to me, over a memory we were disputing (picture this in the most patronising tones you can possibly imagine): 'Now, Danu. You're a fiction writer. And you're a *very good* writer. But it does mean that you have a *very* vivid imagination.'

How do you win against that? How can you prove that just because you write fiction you're not psychotic? You can't.

The narcissistic mothers don't care what evidence you have. I once said that my husband had also heard her say such-a-thing, and she said, slowly and carefully, as to a child, 'Now, Danu. He is your husband. And he loves you very, *very* much. So of course he's going to support what you say.'

Even better, Laura from the DONM forum, relates the time she showed her mother her mother's own signature, and the mother still denied she'd signed the document. Laura said, 'But that is your signature, right?' And her mother said, 'Oh yes. But I didn't sign it.'

This kind of wilful stupid denial is so bizarre and slippery that it's impossible to deal with. Especially since, if you persist in stating your truth (i.e. the real truth), she's likely to move to other defensive tactics such as Narcissistic Rage. And you, programmed from birth to fear her rage, will back down immediately. So when she doesn't confuse you into compliance, she bullies you into it.

She invalidates you.

If she doesn't gaslight you by insisting the event didn't happen, she has another trick. She can admit it happened, but insist that she was right to do so and you are wrong for getting upset. So: 'Well, dear, you *are* getting a bit portly, aren't you? And I had to say it then so you wouldn't have that cake. And your friends didn't mind me saying it, they're well used to your lack of self-control.'

Wonderful – she insists she was right to do it, *and* gets another zinger in at the same time.

Or she might admit she did it, but totally dismiss it. 'Oh seriously, darling, can't you take a joke?' Or, a classic favourite: 'Oh you are *so* sensitive! *Everything* upsets you. It's like walking on eggshells being around you.'

Invalidation is about dismissing your experiences, thoughts and above all your emotions. Indeed the intention is to not even allow you to have those thoughts, experiences and emotions. It's a way of invading your head and reprogramming it. It's psychological abuse (messing with your thoughts) and emotional abuse (messing with your feelings).

I cannot over-stress the enormity of this. To deny someone's feelings or experiences it to literally deny their reality. And that's what happens to we DONMs all the time. The only reality that is allowed to exist is our mother's reality. And where her version of reality clashes with ours, ours must yield.

It's awful. It's beyond awful.

One example from my own experience is when I, miserable because of ongoing infertility, heard that my cousin had had an unplanned pregnancy without being married. (Oh the *schadenfreude* my mother got out of that one as she gleefully shared the news with me!) I said sadly, 'I'd rather be in her shoes than mine', and my mother briskly and dismissively told me, 'No you wouldn't,' and carried on with what she was saying.

Other ways to invalidate include statements like:

- You're over-sensitive (i.e. the fact that this upset you is because you're over-sensitive; it was not inherently upsetting).
- Oh, nothing ever pleases you.
- We have to walk on eggshells around you.
- Don't be like that.
- No, you don't feel that
- Oh you're not *still* going on about that are you? That was *ages* ago.
- You keep bearing grudges.
- Stop crying, or I'll give you something to cry for.
- Oh you always take everything up wrong.
- You're always looking for the worst interpretation.
- Stop feeling so sorry for yourself.
- You're such a moaner / complainer / whinger.
- No one else complains about this.
- I *do* listen to you!
- I *did* show enough interest in your big news.
- You just can't take a joke, can you?
- Lighten up, I was only *teasing*!
- You're so judgemental.
- You're not exactly perfect yourself, are you?
- You're over-reacting. You always over-react.
- You took it up wrong.
- I / she didn't mean it like that.
- I'm sick of you always complaining.
- Well you contributed to it by doing X.
- You've upset me now by saying that.
- It's your fault I did it.
- You made me do it.
- I did it for your own good!
- You have such a poor memory.
- You're just delusional.
- I'm your mother, you need to respect me.

She rages at you.

If neither gaslighting nor invalidation work, and you persist on calling her on whatever she did, she may well go next to an absolute explosion of fury. Or she might just start with that. This fury is known as *Narcissistic Rage.* It just means the way narcissists can explode in absolute, terrifying, rage when they feel threatened in any way. And it does not take much to threaten them. If we take it that narcissists are emotionally still in the toddler stage, then narcissistic rage is nothing more nor less than a toddler tantrum. But it can be hard enough dealing with a genuine toddler's tantrum; dealing with an adult in that same tantrum, especially if / when you're a child yourself, is beyond terrifying.

When she rages no insult, no cruelty, no character assassination is too much to include. She hurls abuse at you and tells you that you are an awful person, that you have no right to have any opinion on anyone's else's foibles when you are just the nastiest person ever and she is so good to even put up with you. And look at this mistake you made, and that bad judgement? And you *dare* to criticise her?

In vain do you try to stay calm, to use 'I' sentences, to share how you feel, to help her understand. In vain do you offer understanding of her situation and maybe even compromises. In vain do you try to keep up with her lightning changes of subject and attacks from different angles, until your brain feels it's going to pop with confusion and frustration.

The problem is that you and she have different aims. Yours is to sort out this issue. Hers is to put you most emphatically back in your box.

Nothing ever gets resolved.

Depending on how vicious the row was, there might be silence between you for a while – a few days or even weeks. During this time she might well be waiting for you to get back to her and apologise, even though you did nothing wrong. But in her mind you did; you attacked her. She is, in her mind, punishing you for your misbehaviour with the worst punishment she can think of: her absence. And even though part of you might relish the peace, the other part of you might be terrified and stressed and upset by it, and really need to get things back to normal. And so you, well trained, might even end up contacting her and apologising.

But if you do not, after a while she will contact you as if there was never any row, with no acknowledgement that any time has passed. She'll send a cheery message: 'Hi, I was wondering how you're doing. I got lots of jam made. And the dog got a sore foot but she's fine now. Give me a call some time.'

And you're left wondering … what? Did you *dream* the row you had the last time you spoke?

This, of course, leaves you in a classic narcissistic no-win situation. Because you are left either having to play the game by her rules, and pretend all is okay, and answer her message on face value, and that means she's getting away with her previous behaviour.

Or you say to her, 'Hang on, Mum, remember the last time we spoke? We need to sort that out first', and end up exposed to the edges of another Narcissistic Rage: 'Are you *still* going on about that? God you're a terrible one for bearing a grudge entirely. That was in the past, and here you are still going on about it. I can do nothing right for you.'

And so, somehow, *you* end up being the bad guy, the unreasonable one, while she gets to play the victim card … how did that happen?

The fact is that they are the ones being unfair. It *is* appropriate to want to sort out a row before moving on. To find out why it happened, and negotiate to do your best that it doesn't happen again. What is not appropriate is, if the situation was sorted out and the person genuinely apologised, to keep mentioning it. That *would* be bearing a grudge. But that is not this situation.

In practice what normally happens is that we DONMs learn well not to rock the boat, and we just accept her cues, and respond as if it were a normal situation. Which of course is what she wants.

She ruins your special days and dismisses your successes.

Narcissistic mothers absolutely hate and resent your special days and successes. This makes sense when you think about it. Since everything is about her, then *your* graduation, *your* pregnancy, *your* baby, *your* book deal, *your* wedding, is almost a crime against nature. You're trying to make it about you, when everything should always be about *her*.

I think that practically every single married member of our forum has her own wedding horror story, and you probably do too. The details vary, but they all have their roots in the narcissistic mother: a) trying to ruin her daughter's joy, and b) trying to get the attention off the bride and back to *her* where it should be.

And if they cannot garner the attention, you may be sure they're not happy. Amanda from our forum relates how she hadn't noticed at the time, but in every one of her sister's baby shower photos, her mother has those pursed lips and glowering expression of the classic Narcissistic Huff.

Now, dismissing our successes does not mean that they cannot at the same time claim them and get attention for them. You may be sure her friends and acquaintances hear *all* about your graduation, your baby, your book deal, your wedding. Because then *she* is getting the attention and maybe even the kudos, the subtext being that it's *her* daughter who's doing so well.

Narcissistic mothers will go as far as to sabotage their daughters' success. The lift you need for the job interview somehow doesn't materialise, for example. Or she might look at the paintings you're going to offer to the gallery and dismiss them. 'They're *quite* nice', she might say dismissively, and part of you dies and you don't even bring them to the gallery to show them there.

But she loves your tragedies.

Well, she loves them *and* she hates them.

She hates them because, again, your tragedies are about you and everything has to be about her. So she can be downright callous and dismissive. 'Get over the miscarriage already, the baby was probably deformed anyway.'

Or she'll trump you. 'Get over your miscarriage already. I had three of them, so why are you complaining about one?'

Or she'll trump you another way. Marianne was told not to inflict her upset about her stillborn baby on her mother, 'Because I'm even more upset than you. I've lost a grandchild *and* I'm worried about your grief. You only have yourself to think about.'

Or what about the classic, 'Oh, you just got a diagnosis of cancer, did you? Sorry to hear that. Which reminds me, my appointment to get my adenoids done is coming up. I tell you, I'll be glad when they're done …' and cue half an hour of talking about her adenoids, and your cancer never mentioned again.

But having said all that, in another way our narcissistic mothers *love* our tragedies and disasters. They get a real Narcissistic Glow going on when anything bad happens to us (or happens to anyone, actually). I believe there are two elements to this: they love the drama, and they love the Narcissistic Supply they'll get from their friends about it.

This can sometimes be funny. My car was stolen from outside my house one night, by so-called joy-riders. They crashed it in a ditch and abandoned it. It was found by a kind man who searched inside and found an envelope addressed to me at my parents' address, and this is how my mother got involved.

She was so excited about this I can't tell you. Total Narcissistic Glow. She was having the time of her life! She was excited, talking quickly, about plans. She and my father would come over to my house that evening to collect me and bring me to collect the car. Fair enough, good plan. She said, 'I don't think there'll be room for John [my husband] though. Not with you and me and Dad and your sister and Millie in the car.'

I should point out that Millie was their massive dog. She wanted to bring the whole family, including the dog, to this event. I tell you, my mother would have been in the front row, knitting furiously, at the French guillotine.

Never mind that the dog's presence precluded that of my husband, who was a) my support that I wanted with me at such a time, and b) the only one of the lot of us who knew anything about cars and therefore was the single most essential person to go.

But usually it's not funny. A young woman died tragically in my mother's town. I heard of it when I went to visit her and she said, in that Narcissistic Glow quivering-with-excitement way, 'I've got some bad news for you!' And proceeded to tell me all about it. And show me the half-page article about it that she had cut out of the local paper, and the paragraph-sized article she'd cut out of the national paper.

She went to the funeral because she knew the woman's aunt somewhat and her mother slightly. In itself this was culturally reasonable. What was not reasonable, and made me literally sick to my stomach, was the totally inappropriate the way she said, glowing like a firefly, 'Oh and *both* her mother and aunt recognised me! And her aunt made a point of coming up to me and telling me I was so good to come!'

This was before I realised about NPD but even so I so wanted to tell her, 'It wasn't about you', but I knew that would get me a dose of Narcissistic Rage, so I said nothing, to my shame. I felt like a silent collaborator in her voyeurism of this tragedy.

She creates Scapegoats and Golden Children.

Some narcissistic mothers divide their children into two categories – that of Scapegoats who can do no right, and Golden Children who can do no wrong.

Being the Scapegoat:

Growing up as the scapegoat is painful and confusing. Why are you always in trouble, when your sibling never gets into trouble for anything? Why can you not get any of your needs met, while your sibling is showered with attention and material possessions? Why are you always blamed for everything?

If you are the Scapegoat you might well become what's known as the Identified Patient (IP) of the family. The IP is the person who is subconsciously selected to carry all the problems of the family, to manifest them. So you, as the IP, might be the one with eating disorders, truancy problems, drinking or drugs, inappropriate sexual behaviour. And you are blamed for all the other troubles in the family, because you're putting everyone under such stress.

You will, no doubt, believe this label. After all, the facts are true, you *do* have these problems. This leads to more feelings of being broken, and is further invalidation.

Your narcissistic mother might even put you into therapy for this. This may, or may not, work in your favour. If the therapist is good enough then s/he will identify what's really going on, and will possibly even label your mother's NPD for you. Alternatively a bad therapist will continue the myth that you are the source of the problems, and be yet another person to invalidate you.

Even if you don't get brought to therapy, it will be 'known' in the family that you are the problem child, the difficulty, the source of stress and upset.

It is no fun being the Scapegoat.

Being the Golden Child:

However, the Scapegoat is, I believe, the lucky one. Well, comparatively lucky – no child of a narcissistic mother is lucky. The Scapegoat is far more likely to seek answers and find them, to escape from the narcissistic web.

The Golden Child can stay trapped in that gilded cage for her whole life, being the narcissistic mother's plaything in effect. The Golden Child is usually engulfed, and her life can end up being very enmeshed with her mother's. On the surface the Golden Child and her mother look to have a very good, and close, relationship. Outsiders might even remark upon it and even envy it. The Scapegoat may even envy it herself and wish she could be as close to their mother.

But it's not a healthy relationship. It's enmeshed. The individual boundaries are blurred beyond recognition.

Note, too, that the Scapegoat role and Golden child role can vary depending on the narcissistic mother's whim. It can even be the same person on different days, which is *very* confusing and leads to total head-wreckingness.

She parentifies.

Narcissistic mothers can apply a process called parentification to their children. This means that she will expect her daughter to act as her (the mother's) parent, to provide comfort to her, to be a sounding board. So the mother might share age-inappropriate (or even just inappropriate) information with her daughter, like details about the mother's own sex life, or details about her romantic relationships, or money worries.

She infantilises.

As a corollary to that, and very possibly existing at the same time, the narcissistic mother might infantalise her daughter in order to keep her weak and trapped, thinking she is dependent on her mother. She may exaggerate the dangers of the world, for example. Or not teach her daughter any of the skills she'll need to survive in the world such as budgeting.

She never apologises.

Narcissistic mothers never apologise. Not properly. Again, it's because in their own minds they are perfect and never do anything wrong, and so there is nothing to apologise for. If called on some inappropriate behaviour they will try gaslighting and invalidating to deflect the accusation. If, however, that fails, they may possibly be forced into the patented narcissists' *fauxpology*™·

This false apology takes a variety of forms. There is the classic 'I'm sorry you got upset', and its rare cousin, 'I'm sorry if I upset you'. Or, the invalidation masquerading as apology: 'I'm sorry that you can't take a joke'.

Or you might get a sarcastic, eye-rolling, 'Sorr-eeee!' in the manner (appropriately) of six year olds being forced to say the word but not meaning a word of it.

The flaw in those is this: Each one is pretending to be an apology, but despite the word 'sorry' appearing in it, it's actually a criticism of *you*! Either a direct criticism, or an implied one.

And if you say it doesn't sound very sincere you will be met with Narcissistic Rage and more gaslighting. Maybe, 'Oh *nothing* ever pleases you! I said sorry, what more do you want? Flesh?'

And you know, deep down, that it's not an apology. But yet it sounds, on the surface, like an apology. And this inconsistency is another part of the crazy-making, head-wreckingness of dealing with a narcissist.

Here is the anatomy of a proper apology: 'I did X. I should not have done it. I apologise without excuse. I will do Y to make amends and/or make sure it doesn't happen again.' There may be reasons given, because most people are careless rather than malicious, but those reasons will not trump the apology. So, 'I'm sorry I forgot your birthday. I was so distracted in work. But still, that doesn't excuse it. Can I bring you out to dinner to make up? And I'll put it in my organiser so I'll be sure to be reminded next year.'

You will *never* hear a Narcissist say baldly, 'I was wrong'.

Once she has fauxpologised she will totally expect things to continue as before. For her, this fauxpology is a kind of Get Out Of Jail Free card. She doesn't see it as meaning that she has to either make amends, or take steps to avoid the behaviour in future.

Now, *you* apologising to a narcissist works totally differently, needless to say.

Quite often, the narcissist will not accept your apology. Why should she? While you're apologising you are in the position of a supplicant. And she gets to lord it over you. Which is a lovely position for a narcissist to be in. Why would she want to allow that wonderful situation to end?

And so you might hear, 'Sorry isn't good enough.' Or, one of my own mother's favourites, a snapped, 'You should have been sorry *before* you did it.' (Even as a child I knew the logic was wrong there.)

Or: 'You will keep apologising until *I* decide that you have apologised enough. And *I* will decide if your apology is sincere or not.'

Knowing what you know now, you won't be surprised that the narcissist will love the one-upmanship of being in this situation, and you're more than likely to witness some major Narcissistic Glow in this case.

Nothing is ever her fault.

Okay, sometimes they'll admit to having done whatever. Maybe it's impossible to deny. But guess what, it won't be their fault that they're doing it! Of course not, they're perfect, so if they fail it must be some other reason rather than any flaw in them. Classic example: my parents both wanted to stop smoking. My father succeeded and my mother did not. Her explanation: 'Well, your father managed to stop because I was so very patient with him during his cranky stage. But I could not stop because he got cross and impatient when I was struggling.'

Or my mother's assertion that she talks too much only because I make her nervous. Or that she never shows interest in my stuff because whatever she does, it's not right by me and so she's too tense to react normally.

She has a victim/martyr mentality.

Narcissists are always victims, never perpetrators. They see themselves as being frequently attacked and are therefore justified in defending themselves. And how do you attack them? By calling them on their behaviour, no matter how mildly you do it. If you say, 'Mum, I would prefer that you didn't do X in future as it upsets me', you will get a reaction which would be more appropriate if you had said, 'I'm going to kill your pets, burn your house down and torture you for days'. Truly, that's how it feels to narcissists. Putting a boundary in place feels like an attack on them. Disagreeing with them is tantamount to grievously injuring them.

Every event is twisted into some victimisation of her. It's amazing how much she will twist the truth and leave out facts to play the martyr.

And, in an exquisite irony, she will have her acolytes, and her co-dependent family members (of which more below), to rally around and give her sympathy for her nasty ungrateful daughter being so mean and nasty to her.

Which further validates that *she* was right and you are wrong, because everyone is agreeing that that's the case.

Which adds to the head-wreckingness of the whole thing for you. You still have the original upset, and now you have it invalidated and dismissed, and in addition, somehow *you're* the bad guy?

And, finally, another way of being the martyr and using that to bring you into line is the trump card of, 'Oh, after all I have sacrificed for you!' You are reminded how she gave up her big career for you, how much your education cost, how she put herself out to bring you to dance lessons, etc. (Please, please, do not fall for this. It was her decision to become a mother and all of those things were her responsibility as a result of that. You do not owe her anything for giving you what were both legally and morally your rights. You really don't.)

She's vindictive, and operates smear campaigns.

There are four layers to how a narcissist is:

- She first of all wants your admiration. That's her default state. Admire her, listen to her. Agree with her. Worship her even.
- If she doesn't get your admiration, she'd like your fear. This is where Narcissstic Rage comes in.
- Failing that, she wants your pity. She'll play the victim card as discussed above.
- And if even that doesn't work, she moves onto being vindictive and starting a smearing campaign.

Thing is, they can bear grudges *forever*. Again, this makes sense because if they are so special, so perfect, it absolutely is a capital crime to go against them. They are actually dangerous in this respect, because they can wait and bide their time for years to get revenge. And this is why, if you come across a narcissist in your daily life, try to remove yourself with as little drama as possible. Be uninteresting to them is the best advice, and don't engage them and definitely don't take them on.

Smearing is one of their big weapons. Smearing means to bad-mouth you to everyone she possibly can. To start a whispering campaign against you. To spread rumours against you. This has the twin benefit to the narcissist of getting her victim status and lots of sympathy (i.e. Narcissistic Supply) on the one hand, and exacting revenge upon you on the other.

Smearing is very, very hard to counteract. It's all so sly and underhand that you mightn't even realise it's happening. The first you'll know of it is when the friend doesn't speak to you, or is cool with you. When the business contact stops returning your calls. Even when you ask the friend or the business contact what's wrong, they won't tell you. You may be sure the narcissist has anticipated that, and has dealt with it in some way ('Don't tell her what I said').

She never allows you to be your authentic self.

Whenever I pulled up outside my parents' house, I sat for a moment before getting out of the car. And in that moment I could feel myself folding my true authentic Self away. What went into their house was effectively a cardboard cut-out that looked exactly like me, but was not 'me' in any real sense. Because, I had learned over many years that the real authentic true me was not welcome. The real me was not approved of, or even tolerated. They wanted the pretty image of me who listened to their stories, never had needs of her own, never rocked the boat, never challenged. The one who played into the fantasy that we were happy families with a happy and healthy and well-functioning relationship.

Not allowing your authentic self to exist is effectively soul murder.

She triangulates.

Narcissists like to be the centre of operations, the controller of information. And therefore they often operate a process called *triangulation*, which means that all information goes through them. So they'll discourage you from speaking to your siblings, and instead tell you all you need to know about their news. And of course, in doing this they can spin the information to suit themselves and even tell outright lies. This can mean that you and your siblings (or other important people) become estranged as each is told lies about the other. This suits the narcissist perfectly as you cannot then collaborate or conspire against her. 'Divide and Conquer' is her motto.

She probably loves her illnesses.

Many narcissists experience, and seem to love, a variety of non life-threatening illnesses. These illnesses require medical attention and therefore provide Narcissistic Supply for them, as well as making it necessary for family members to run around looking after them, listening to them talk about their illnesses, make allowances for the illnesses, etc. There is a disorder called Munchausen's Syndrome which is similar to this. I have not found any official link, or understanding of a link, between that and NPD. But it does seem that narcissists do use illnesses for attention.

She is odd about gifts and presents.

Narcissistic mothers are very strange about presents. They are *dreadful* at buying presents for people around them, usually getting the most inappropriate gifts imaginable. This is for two reasons: first, they genuinely don't know anyone as a person, so they've no idea what they'd like. And second, they really don't care. If they were to start thinking about stuff like that, they'd have to take time out from thinking of themselves and that, of course, cannot be.

And so you have the most bizarre examples of presents: the clothes in a style you'd never wear, the book on a hobby you've never shown the slightest interest in, a voucher for something you'd absolutely hate. And of course the sigh and the comment, 'Oh you're *so* hard to buy for', if she feels your lack of enthusiasm.

They're great at re-gifting, too, and again it doesn't matter if the gift is appropriate for you, or how tatty its box is, or how obvious it has been pulled out at the last minute from the back of the cupboard.

There is, however, one occasion on which they'll put thought into a present, and that's when it's a veiled dig. The diet book. The book on getting your home organised. Those they can do.

In a seeming paradox, but one which makes sense, they actually love *the act* of giving presents. I recall well the vivid Narcissistic Glow my mother would have whenever she handed over a gift. This is because it was expected that the recipient would show huge, if not fawning, gratitude. Lots of Narcissistic Supply, in other words. The gift donor is also in a slightly higher position, status-wise, as they are the ones able to bestow resources, and she likes being in that position. And then you'd have to hear the story, in excruciating detail, about how she came to buy that gift.

Regardless of what kind of present you get therefore, you absolutely *must* show huge gratitude or face Narcissistic Rage. The fuss and compliments must go on long after any reasonable person would expect, and must be fulsome and repetitive. They don't have to be sincere, mind. Narcissists aren't very good at detecting sincerity or its lack (again because they'd have to think about someone else to do so, and also in their arrogance they never assume that the other person wouldn't mean it).

And in a logical corollary, you won't be shocked to hear that they react badly to receiving presents. They can be dismissive and just say a casual, 'Thanks' as they toss it to one side. Or they can be downright vicious (or tearful, if that works better) as they turn on you for buying something so beneath them or wrong for them.

She might hate your partner.
But she might not ...

Here's the thing. She wants you weak and scared and isolated and vulnerable. She does not want you to be strong and empowered. So if you get together with a partner who empowers you and supports you and is good to you, she may well hate that, and may do all in her power to sabotage that relationship. Get together with a narcissist or other abuser though, and she's quite happy ....

She has no boundaries.
Narcissists often see no boundaries at all. It's not at all unheard of for the narcissistic mother to let herself into her daughter's house and start re-arranging the kitchen cupboards. Or ask – and expect answers to – totally inappropriate questions about topics such as your sex life, family planning decisions or finances. Or share equally inappropriate information about themselves.

They see this as totally their right. And so they feel very thwarted and angry if you try to stop them doing it, if you try to impose natural and reasonable boundaries.

Because, thing is, narcissists *hate* boundaries. Hate them with a passion. They actually experience boundaries as being an attack on them, and will respond to that attack with huge force and Narcissistic Rage. And will consider it totally justified, just as you would be justified to use all possible force against a physical attacker.

And so if you say, for example, 'Mum, I'd really prefer it if you'd phone before coming around, rather than just turning up', then she sees that as an attack and will respond accordingly.

She may get offended, or just go straight to rage.

She might accuse you of emotional blackmail, and may say that in such a way that you begin to wonder if it is.

She might say, 'Fine! I won't visit at all, then, I know when I'm not wanted!' and in vain will you protest that that's *not* what you said or what you meant.

She might get upset, and start sobbing, 'Nothing I ever do is right! My own daughter doesn't want me!' And you end up comforting her and assuring her that of course she does things right, and of course you want her. And so the focus of the discussion gets efficiently moved *from* your request *to* her upset, and it never moves back.

Or she might go on the attack: 'Well it's a bit rich *you* asking people to have manners. What about all the times you turned up on *my* doorstep, eh?' In vain do you try to remind her that she had insisted you do that, that you tried to ring first but she didn't want that.

And of course, she might then smear you to anyone who'll listen, totally twisting the truth to suit her scenario: 'My daughter told me I wasn't to visit her any more!'

And if you think that such a dramatic response was an over-reaction to your mild request for her to ring before visiting – well, you'd be right. But because narcissists are so hyper-sensitive to *any* suggestion that they're less than perfect, this dramatic response was, to her, *totally* justified. Your mild suggestion really was a brutal attack, to her.

And yes, there's an irony here. As part of the invalidation, she accuses you of being over-sensitive, when the reality is that she is the one who is completely over-sensitive.

We will talk more about setting boundaries with narcissists on page 85.

It's always about her needs.

In a relationship with a narcissist, it's always about meeting her needs, and never about getting your own needs met. This is, of course totally contrary to what the mother-child relationship should be, where it's about the mother meeting the child's appropriate needs.

If you have an Ignoring Mother as I did, she will not expect you to meet her needs so much – my own mother was always pretty self-sufficient and didn't require much from either me or my siblings. But she wasn't interested in meeting our needs, beyond the minimum that she had to.

Engulfing Mothers, now, are an endless whirlwind of needs, and so the daughter grows up trying to meet her needs, and unaware that her own needs should be met, and never getting them met

So, even as she totally demands her own needs (and even her *wants*), she makes you feel selfish for looking to meet your own needs. So, for example, if you wanted *this* dress or *that* venue, for your wedding, but she preferred another one, you'll get told, either indirectly or in as many words: 'Oh you're so selfish, you know. It's not all about you. You always want your own way. You never think of anyone else.' And so you end up feeling really bad about being so selfish, and more than likely giving in to her wishes.

She lies to you about who you are.

It is a parent's job is to reflect the child to him- or herself, so they grow up with an appropriate self-image. Narcissists twist that and they lie to us about who we are. They teach us that we are inherently flawed and there is something sinister and wrong about us. Much more about this huge topic on pages 56 – 57.

She is very sensitive.

Narcissistic mothers are also very, very sensitive to criticism. In one of many ironies that narcissism lends itself to, she may accuse you of being over-sensitive and requiring that she walk on eggshells, but the truth is exactly the opposite – she is that very thing! Her ego is so fragile that she's always on guard for any slights to it, and will react with all due force, i.e. Narcissistic Rage, to it.

For example, I remember when my mother, a devout Catholic, said, totally seriously, about some Protestants she'd met, 'And they had a very good sense of humour for Protestants', I couldn't help it, I laughed. I said, 'Mother, your prejudices are showing!' Cue a clipped, 'That's enough, Danu!' And I, indoctrinated from birth, crawled docilely back into my box.

However, narcissistic mothers are very quick to criticise others. As everything is about her, she can have this odd way in which she takes others' differing opinions or tastes as a personal affront to her. She doesn't merely disagree with them, rather she is *offended* by them. This makes sense in that backwards narcissistic way, as, since she's perfect, her opinion and tastes are the right ones and the others' are wrong. And worse, by having those different opinions and tastes, the others are implicitly criticising hers! No wonder she's offended.

She talks a lot. A lot!

Talking a lot can be a trait of Histrionic Personality Disorder, specifically, but many narcissists seem to have this too. After all, if she's the Centre of the Universe then her every passing thought is of enough importance to share with the world, and every detail of her life is essential listening.

Narcissists can talk endlessly about their own events and opinions, in the most excruciating detail. They talk on and on and on until it feels like an assault. They can talk without drawing breath it seems like. This has the result of making you, the designated audience, feel like a non-person. You're only there as their audience, not as a real person. I always used to feel, going into my mother's presence, that I was folding the real me away, and what went to see her was a cardboard cut-out that looked like me, but it was not, in any real sense, me. The real me was totally surplus to requirements.

Once, in an experiment, I sat and listened to my mother without giving any response cues at all. I just sat and stared at her. She began talking about a holiday she and my father had just been on, even though they had both had already spent a good hour or so telling me about it. But no matter, she spoke again about it. And no word of exaggeration as I timed it on the oven clock, but she spoke solidly for forty full minutes, with zero encouragement from me, about a holiday she had literally just told me all about.

She's a master of projection.

'Projection' in this context means the psychological tendency to see one's undesirable traits in another. And narcissists cannot, of course, bear to own their undesirable traits, so they have to get rid of them, so to speak, as soon as possible. So they hand them to the nearest recipient who'll take them. And their children are of course very handy for this, as they unquestioningly believe their parents.

So they'll accuse you of being what they dimly realise they are being, but they cannot cope with the pain of that, so they'll project it on to you.

Calling you over-sensitive when it's actually they who are over-sensitive is one such example. Calling you selfish. Telling you that you can't tell truth from reality. And so it goes.

The scary thing is that, of course, we believe it when we hear it. As children, we're programmed to believe our parents, and so we grow up thinking we *are* selfish and greedy and all the bad things she accuses us of. It's more of the head-wreckingness. And of course, when she says we can't tell truth from reality, the evidence is there as we remember things differently to her. Truly, what chance have we, as little children, got against this?

She probably mismanaged your appearance.

When you're a child, your appearance, hair, cleanliness, and clothing will all be impacted by the whims and needs of your narcissistic mother.

If she's an Ignoring Mother then your appearance will most likely be neglected. This was so in my case. I was, frankly, dirty, although I am mortally embarrassed to write this. My long thick hair was mostly unbrushed and tangled. In fact the only times I remember my mother touching me in my childhood was on the rare occasions she brushed my hair to get the tangles out, and it was a time of great fury and frustration and rage at me for the state of my hair, and great pain for me as she tugged mercilessly. But this was at an age, maybe 8 or 9, when I truly should not, could not, have been responsible for its upkeep, especially since I was never taught self-care. I also remember wearing the same vest for months upon months until it was literally grey. I had tide marks around my neck and ears. I remember aged 12 wearing slippers to school because I had no shoes. We weren't rich, but we had money for shoes. No one had noticed my shoes were unwearable, and I, for some reason, did not say.

Other Narcissistic Mothers proactively make their daughters ugly, fearing the competition. Shelly recalls how her mother insisted on her having a boy's haircut, and how she hated it and pleaded and begged to be allowed to grow it, but was forbidden. Others are bought the most hideous clothes, designed to do the opposite of flatter. This form of the abuse can often kick in, not surprisingly, at the time of the daughter's puberty, but it can also be life-long.

Still others, however, dress their daughters perfectly. Too perfectly perhaps. They dress them like little dolls. Not surprisingly it's often Engulfing Mothers who do this. These daughters are put into overly pretty dresses, their hair tortured into complex styles, and they are never allowed to wear shorts and climb trees.

Others are dressed very well, and even appropriately, but it's because it's part of the image of the Perfect Family the parents wish to project. Perfect grooming is part of this dynamic.

Ordinary healthy cleanliness, which allows for getting dirty in play, but being cleaned after that, does not seem to apply to any of these families.

She may neglect your medical care.
It often happens that narcissistic mothers don't get appropriate medical care for their children. I have heard so many horror stories of bones not set in time, of scars remaining where wounds did not get stitched and so on. Dentists' visits and other maintenance type of medical care can often be neglected too.

She might make you overly dependent too young.
Narcissistic mothers often don't bother to teach their daughters the skills they need to look after themselves, e.g. personal care, and they don't necessarily look after their daughters' care either. The other extreme is that they expect their daughters to be responsible for themselves way too early in life. Anne remembers having to use the washing machine before she was tall enough to even easily reach the buttons.

She probably has zero curiosity.
Narcissists have zero genuine curiosity. Oh, for sure they might have nosiness. Especially if they can nose out something to your detriment or their benefit. Or if they can find out something about a celebrity which makes them feel more important for knowing it. But genuine curiosity about you, or anyone else – nope. They don't care about your fears (except to exploit them), hopes (except to dash them), desires (except to mock them, or get the same thing for themselves).

She's sly.
She says cruel things to you when no one is around, or coded things when they are. She phrases her insults as concern for you. She manipulates with gifts and help. So no one else sees the cruelty. They

may well think she's lovely. This adds to the isolation and feeling of being crazy.

She probably will be vain.

You might be surprised that it has taken this long for a narcissist's vanity to be mentioned. Vanity is, after all, the very first thing people think of when they think of narcissism. They often equate vanity and narcissism. However, narcissism is far more than vanity, and might not even include vanity.

But having said that, narcissists can of course be vain. Typically they tend to be vain either about their looks, and these we call somatic narcissists, or about their intelligence, and these we call cerebral narcissists.

It is important to stress that in neither case does the narcissist have to actually *be* exceptionally beautiful or intelligent. She just has to believe herself to be this. As already explained, narcissists have a fairly relaxed relationship with the truth anyway, so this is just one more aspect to that.

She rarely cries genuine tears.

Only tears of self-pity or rage, or false tears to manipulate you. Not tears like we would: tears of grief or upset or sadness for others.

She doesn't genuinely mourn.

Except for her own loss. So a narcissist who loses her husband will mourn what that'll mean for her life. But she won't mourn her husband for himself. Still less will she feel bad about him, that he has died.

She has no sense of humour.

Narcissists have no sense of humour beyond, sometimes, a slapstick slipping-on-banana-skin humour. They can never, ever take a joke against themselves, which of course makes sense too, right? But they can often miss the subtleties of all kinds of humour, because a lot of it depends on empathy. We laugh because we feel for the butt of the joke – but narcissists never feel for anyone but themselves and so they don't get the joke.

She probably loves prestige.

Sometimes they'll just claim it, by assuming they're more important than everyone else (and it's surprising how much other people buy into that). Other times they'll get it by being holier-than, or helpier-than, anyone else. Sometimes people who are very active in prominent roles – church, community associations, charities etc, are getting Narcissistic Supply from this. Of course, not all such people are. There are many, many genuine people there too. But the ones who are prominent, who get seen, they might well be narcissistic.

And it might include your mother. Which helps with the crazy-makingness of it all. Here is everyone else telling you how *wonderful* she is, how helpful, and yet you are the one emotionally bruised and upset every time you deal with her. Trying to reconcile those twin realities can be truly head-wrecking. One clue is to look out for Narcissistic Glow. The genuine helpers will get pleasure from it, sure, and it's human to like being appreciated. But they won't have that Narcissistic Glow going on.

She may blame you for getting in the way of some huge success.

One trick that some narcissistic mothers do is to claim some lost, would-be huge success which was in her grasp but she had to give it up raise her children, i.e. you. So she was accepted to RADA but turned it down when she got pregnant. Or won a regional singing competition, but couldn't take it further for the same reason.

This is actually a pretty superb trick. She gets the kudos of being a wonderful actor or singer without ever having to prove herself at it or risk failure and rejection, *and* she gets to use it as a stick to beat her children with. 'After all I sacrificed for you!' would be the refrain there.

She has no introspection.

Narcissists are never introspective.

They never analyse their actions or motivations. Things just *are,* and by definition, since it's the Narcissist doing it, are appropriate. They don't need to think any further about it.

And so you'll never get a narcissist pondering ruefully about some past mistake, or sharing a lesson she learned, or laughing at something embarrassing they did.

And so it's like they are petrified in amber, emotionally speaking. They never learn. They never grow. They never mature.

Most of us like to think of life as a journey of growth and increasing awareness and increasing maturity. We like to learn from our mistakes so we don't make them again. We like to improve our life skills all the time, including our relationship skills.

Not narcissists. How can you improve on perfection? And so narcissists are the same at 50 as they were at 20. They do not gather wisdom or maturity.

She takes everything personally.

Very personally. Everything is about how it impacts on her, or reflects on her. And so, if you hold a different opinion to her, it can literally *offend* her. Again, given what we know about how narcissists think they're perfect in every way, that makes sense. If they think blue is the nicest colour, then it is. And therefore if you think red is a nicer colour, a) you're wrong, and b) you're subliminally suggesting that *she* is wrong to prefer blue and this is back to being an attack on her.

The concept that colour preferences are simply that – a preference, and that no one is right or wrong, does not occur to them.

And I picked such a trivial example as colour on purpose, because even such a trivial example will offend a narcissist. And so, whatever you do, don't express a different opinion on something major like religion or politics.

She lies against all the evidence.

Have you ever had the experience of a four- or five-year-old child looking you straight in the eye, and *swearing* with total sincerity that they were nowhere near the biscuit jar, despite the chocolate smeared all over their faces? You might even point out the fact of the chocolate stains and they'll insist that, even so, they didn't eat the biscuits. They make no attempt, even, to explain the chocolate. Without shame they'll acknowledge that there's chocolate on their face, but still insist that that they didn't eat the biscuits.

That's the sort of thing narcissists do. They just dismiss all evidence that doesn't fit in with their story. They may refuse to acknowledge the evidence exists, in classic gaslighting. Or they might acknowledge the evidence is there but refuse to acknowledge that that proves anything. Laura relates how her narcissistic mother quite happily said, 'Yes, that's my signature on that document, but it wasn't me that signed it'.

Where do you go with that? Logic does no good at all as they will just keep denying.

She's inappropriate with service staff.

I did a survey on my forum about this, and it was as I suspected. Narcissists are often very inappropriate with service staff and others who they see as being beneath them. They can either be imperious and rude, or else over-familiar.

ENABLING FATHERS

We need to speak, too, of Enabling Fathers.

There are only three possible fathers for a DONM: another narcissist (oh yes, that can happen; lucky the DONM who has that), an absent father, or an Enabling Father.

An Enabling Father is, as the title suggests, one who enables your narcissistic mother's behaviour. He will not protect you, nor rock the boat to even defend you. He might even proactively assist in her abuse, such as beating you on her command. He might try to ride both horses, whispering to you ruefully, 'Ah, just put up with her, you know how she is', or, 'You have to be the bigger person here', or, 'Forgive and forget'. And because we're raised with this as the default, we don't realise the lack of logic in those statements.

His enabling behaviour can be because he is scared of her too. It is impossible to have a healthy, empowered relationship with a narcissist. This is why many fathers leave. Those who stay are – must be – enmeshed in the co-dependent dysfunctional dynamic.

Or maybe he's not scared of her. Maybe he needs, as is the case, I believe, with my own father, to believe his wife is perfect (because it reflects well on him to have a perfect wife, I guess), and so he and she are both in this toxic conspiracy to present her as perfect. It doesn't mean that he cannot have petty rows with her; he does. But he always sided with her when it came to his children, and indeed he acted as her attack dog when needed.

If a father leaves the marriage, the narcissistic mother can often make it her business to estrange or distance her daughter from the father, bad-mouthing and bitching about him. So the result is that you lose contact with your father.

Right now you might be having some major *aha* moments. And yet, the guilt might be kicking in right about now. How could you *possibly* think this about your mother? You probably feel dreadful for thinking of her like this.

You recall how she is/was nice so often. This is no doubt true. Narcissists are often nice; they can be even charming and pleasant once they get their way. Many narcissistic mothers are good with small children, and you might have fond memories of her treatment of you before you were about 7, in other words, before you developed your own personality and opinions.

The thing is that all abusers are nice sometimes – see page 71 for more on that. It doesn't justify, or excuse, their bad behaviour.

And your feelings of guilt are just your programmed beliefs. There is much more information on page 120 about this, and you can either go there and read that now, and then come back here. Or, alternatively, just 'park' the feelings of guilt for now, and read on till you get to that section.

3
THE EFFECTS ON US OF BEING RAISED AS THE DAUGHTER OF A NARCISSISTIC MOTHER

We wryly call NPD 'the gift that keeps on giving'. The effects on us, as women who were raised by a narcissist, are seemingly endless.

Before we go into this list, let me acknowledge that it's a fairly depressing list. But there are a few things to keep in mind. The first is that all these issues are totally reasonable and logical reactions to the twisted and abusive upbringing. They're not a sign of anything intrinsically wrong with you. The truth is that:

> *You are not broken in need of fixing.*
> *You are perfectly and wonderfully made.*
> *You are, rather, wounded in need of healing.*

But yet, there are many issues we do have to deal with. Here's a selection.

We often have problems with perception, and think we're crazy.
Here's the thing: children are programmed at an extremely deep level to believe their parents. This is wired into us by biology, by evolution.

Reason being, the child who believed her parents' comments about danger, without needing to prove it for herself, survived to pass on her genes more than the child who didn't. This system works really well when the parent is well-meaning and telling the truth to protect the child. The system fails when the parents are lying to the child to protect their own self-image or ego.

The result is that you are getting two contradictory pieces of information. The first is what your own perception tells you: what you saw, what you heard, what you experienced. The second is what your mother insists that you saw, heard and experienced.

And given how insistent narcissists can be, combined with our natural propensity to believe our mothers, we come to believe *their* version of events over our own. This truly is head-wrecking.

There is *no* security in a world where we cannot (as we think) trust even our own perceptions. How do we know what reality is, if we cannot (again, as we think) judge it correctly?

We come to think we're crazy. Which is a totally logical thing to think – all the evidence is there, right?

And this, therefore, is the biggest gift, of the many many gifts of realising your mother is narcissistic and has been lying all this time, a gift so pivotal that it forms the title of this book:

> *You are not crazy.*
> *You are perfectly sane.*
> *Your perceptions are valid and right*
> *You can trust your own reality.*

Now, knowing this rationally is one thing. Believing it at a core level is quite another. We talk more about beliefs later in this book, and will deal with that issue then. For now, just park the doubts along with the guilt. Or go to page 120.

It feels like we were born broken.

Many DONMs have a deeply buried sense that we are inherently flawed. That there is something twisted and evil and nasty and noxious and poisonous about us, and that we were born that way. It's part of who we *are* rather than just something we do. This brings with it a huge all-encompassing sense of shame.

This belief is partly us trying to make sense of the fact that even our own mother did not love us, because in a child's logic the mother is perfect, and so if she doesn't love us, it *must* be a flaw in us rather than in her.

But often it's also a direct, if veiled, statement from our mother or parents too. They more or less *tell* us this! They tell us that only they know the real us, and it's not a pretty sight, and only *they* could possibly put up with us, knowing the truth about us. All our friends, they suggest, would abandon us in a heartbeat if they knew what we were *really* like.

This is confusing, because at some level we know we're not *that* bad. But yet, we are accustomed to believing their 'knowledge' over our own perception, so we come to think we *are* that bad, in some vague unspecified way. And this badness is even scarier for being unspecified. How can we fix it or cure it if we don't even know what it is?

I lived in terror of finding out just how broken I was – this awfulness was too big and too dreadful to be even faced up to or acknowledged full-on. And so they were able to keep me docile and quiescent for years with the veiled threat to show me exactly how awful I was. I called it, in my own mind, *The Horrible Danu Mirror*. Once I looked in it, there would be no more hiding. I would know exactly how deformed and grotesque I was. And so I dared not look into the mirror; I dared not let them tell me details of how bad I was. And the threat to show me the mirror kept me compliant for years and years, well into middle-age.

Now I know that there is no such twisted and grotesque 'me'. That the real me is a normally flawed but mostly decent and kind and genuine woman. An ordinary, averagely-nice human being in fact. And coming to realise this is another gift of what I call the N-realisation.

It was, of course, not just me who experienced this toxic emotional blackmail. Many other DONMs do so too.

As Kate says: 'It's utterly cruel. Basically what we're talking about is brainwashing a small child into believing they are fundamentally completely unlikeable, leaving them terrified that someone is going to uncover this fact and therefore living their life pretending in order to cover up some problem they don't even have! As children we were forced to join their cult of fakeness and facade without any clue what is going on.'

As a direct result of this brainwashing, we end up feeling huge all-encompassing shame about who we are. And we carry that shame with us every second of every minute of every day. A constant companion, that we don't even know is there because we're so used to it. But it colours our experience of all elements of life.

In my absolute opinion, this, along with lying to us about our perspective and making us think we're crazy, is the worst element of the abuse they perpetrate against us.

Lisa says: 'It is an awful tool that they use against us. My NM told me that it was easy for me to have friends since I only show them my good side, but the family knows the "whole" me. I have felt split in two for years...the "real" me (the awful, selfish, mean, ungrateful, angry, self-centred one) and the "other" me, the one where I am pretending not to be those other things! Isn't that terrible? The other thing my narcissistic mother would say, to further drive her points and her power over me home ..."I know you better than you know yourself".'

And Miriam experienced the same: 'It's a really sick trick and mind-game to undermine a child's sense of self. The message is "Even if you think you're ok- we know the TRUTH about you".'

We expect our own perfection.
Our Narcissistic Mother told us a Big Lie. She told it subliminally if

not in actual words. And The Big Lie was this: *If we tried hard enough we could win her approval and her love.* If we were good enough, or wise enough, or beautiful enough, or that-magical-unspecified-ingredient enough. In other words, if we achieved perfection, she would love us.

It was a carrot she dangled before us, always.

As part of that lie, any of our normal foibles and failings were treated mercilessly, and were a source of great shame, and even perhaps a way of totally dismissing and invalidating who we were as a person. No wonder it's so hard to accept being wrong.

The thing is, she told us this Big Lie from birth. So of course we believed it. Why wouldn't we?

The interesting thing, though, is that we then enter the conspiracy ourselves. We tell The Big Lie to ourselves.

Why?

Because to let it go leaves us powerless, and we cannot bear to think of that possibility.

If we keep believing The Big Lie then it seems as if the solution is in our hands. And that makes us feel better. The relationship with our mother *can* be fixed. All we have to do is, try harder, behave better, find the magic key, no matter how long it takes to find, or how much energy we devote to the search or what else we're not doing that we could be doing.

The reality, however, is that the solution was never in our hands. There was nothing we could have done to win her love or approval. Withholding those things gave her her power because it kept us clingy and focused on her. So she kept moving the goalposts to make sure we never were perfect enough, or good enough. It was a quintessential no-win game. But we didn't know that.

And so we continue to believe that we have to strive for this elusive perfection, that at some future time we'll succeed. And therefore, we take over where she left off, beating ourselves up for not being perfect. For being human. For making normal human mistakes.

An interesting, albeit challenging, exercise is to make a point of listening to your self-talk. That internal chatter that goes on all the time, but that we're not aware of unless we listen. Try to make a point of tuning in. You may be horrified at how abusive you are to yourself. If you make a little mistake, 'Oh that is so *stupid*! You're *always* doing that. Can't you do *anything* right?'

The trick then is to try to speak kindly to yourself when you hear that chatter. Like you would to your own child. We had a phrase we used with our son whenever he did anything stupid: 'That wasn't your best idea'. It was a way of acknowledging the error without shaming him or identifying his Self with the event. It was so good to hear him, as he got older, identify things the same way: 'Whoops, that wasn't my best idea.' Isn't that a gentler and kinder way than the dialogue above?

So maybe speak to yourself like that. 'That wasn't my best idea. A better idea would be to do it this way.'

Try to come to a place where you accept your own imperfections. Where it's okay to be less than perfect. Because you *are* less than perfect; it's the human condition. And that's okay! That really is okay, no matter that she lied to you and told you differently. You might as well beat yourself up for not being able to fly.

But of course this means you'll never win her love, seeing as you're not perfect.

But you know, that wasn't going to happen anyway. You know that, deep down, even if you understandably struggle to accept it. So you do not have to continue on the toxic hamster wheel, running, running, trying to win her approval but getting nowhere.

You can step off that wheel. You can step off whenever you like.

The price of stepping off is to let go the hope that the relationship can ever be fixed.

The reward is freedom. And energy to do things for *you*. And peace.

(The EFT Script on page 163 will help hugely with this.)

Learning to accept your imperfections can take time, of course.

And so it could still happen that as you read through the rest of this list about the impact on DONMs of having a narcissistic mother, that you'll feel shame and disapproval of yourself for having these issues.

Don't!

Seriously, don't. The thoughts might come, but again, just park them for now. You can't help thinking them, but you can help believing them.

We might be like a bird behind a window.

You know that famous phrase about the definition of madness: It's to keep on doing the same things but expecting a different result.

And we DONMs do that with our mothers. We keep going back to her hoping that *this time* it'll be different. This time she'll be the mother we need her to be. This time she'll support us in our grief, applaud us in our success, be good company with no agenda. This time she'll accept us as we really are, and love us for it.

And she never does.

When I think of this dynamic (which I, too, did for far too many years) I think of a bird flying fruitlessly into a window, again and again.

It breaks my heart. It breaks my heart for me, and for all of us.

I do understand this pattern, and I do forgive myself for doing it, as I hope you can forgive yourself.

We feel we're powerless against her.

DONMs can often be in a state of learned helplessness with regard to our narcissistic mothers. It makes sense since, when we were children, we *were* helpless to protect ourselves. But that no longer applies.

You have more power than you realise. There is nothing they can really do. Their Narcissistic Rage is only toddlers' tantrums, and can be seen as such. Their Narcissistic Huff is just a sulk.

So they have no power really.

Now having said that, narcissists can try tricks. Narcissistic mothers have been known to report their daughters to Social Services for abuse of their (i.e. the daughters') children, just out of spite, for example. But even then, the falseness of the reports were soon exposed and the narcissist's power was gone.

So, be realistic about what she can do. If there is anything, prepare for it as best as you can. But also don't think she can do more than she can.

We usually have self-esteem issues.

Most, if not all, daughters of narcissistic mothers have very low self-esteem. Again, it's not surprising. When you're taught from birth that you don't matter in any way, that your wants and even needs are irrelevant, then of course you'll struggle to value yourself.

Add to that other ways in which you were not valued. If your mother didn't look after your physical well-being or hygiene, what does that tell you about your value? If she never listened to you, what do you learn from that?

If she engulfed you, at some level you learned you didn't even exist as a real separate person.

In a million ways, a million times, you were told and taught and shown that you did not matter and had no value. And you believed it. And you brought that feeling into your adult life.

We have difficulty knowing who we are.

If you grew up with your narcissistic mother telling you who you were, creating you in *her* image, it can be very hard to know who you really are. You might struggle knowing even basic things about yourself such as your tastes in food, clothing, colours.

Shelly came up with this idea: 'One thing that I've had some fun with is an "All About Me!" book. It's just what it sounds like and it feels kind of silly to have, but I've found that it actually has been helping me get to know myself. I write down foods I love or "rules" like: It's always okay to buy extra hand soap. (For some reason, I struggle with buying hand soap of all things—it feels like a "luxury" item to have separate soap at the bathroom sink... weird, I know.) I add notes as I learn things about myself like that I need to drink extra water when I'm out in the car all day or I'll get a massive headache the next day. Just really basic observations, I suppose, but they're things I didn't really notice about myself. And noticing seems to be helping and leading me to notice other things.'

We can lack confidence.

Not all DONMs have this issue. I confess that I was always blessed with an abundance of confidence myself; I have no idea why. But many DONMs struggle with this. They struggle in social situations, in work and so on. I think it has to do with always being judged, and being scared of being judged.

We can have difficulty being assertive.

This is allied to the lack of confidence, and is a huge issue for DONMs. And again it makes sense – if we tried to be assertive with our mothers we were subjected to lies, gaslighting, verbal (and even physical) abuse and shaming. And this translates into our adult lives too. We also have a massive fear of confrontation for the same reasons. And this leads us to put up with treatment that we should not put up with.

One way this can manifest is in difficulty in saying no to requests. Most likely, you were never allowed to say no as a child. And so it can be very difficult to do so as an adult. Again, this takes practice. As an interim step, maybe practise saying, 'Let me have a think about that and get back to you.' No one genuine will have a problem with that, and it'll give you time to consider your options. And then if you don't want to do that, you can say simply, 'I've thought about your request and I'm not in a position to do that. Sorry.' Reasonable people will accept that.

You don't have to give a reason why not, and sometimes it's good not to give a reason. Not to be rude, but simply as practice in not feeling you have to justify yourself. You don't need others to agree or understand why you choose not to do it. Of course, in real life, with reasonable people, it's courtesy to do so. But do be aware that there is no obligation to do that.

And on a related note, it's also possible to change your mind. To say, 'Remember I said I'd do that? Well I'm so sorry, but I've realised I can't after all. Sorry.'

It's better to say no before committing to something, as you don't want to let people down. But if you felt manipulated or pressured, or you simply realised it's too much for you to do, you can always change your mind.

We can tend to end up in bad relationships.

Many DONMs end up with narcissistic partners, and friends. Again, this makes sense when you think about it. It's what we know. It's what we expect from relationships. And the narcissists are drawn to us because they know we'll put up with them.

Another reason why we end up with narcissists (and sometimes other abusers) is because, as already said, our narcissistic mothers tend to be very unhappy if we're involved with good people. They don't want us to be supported, encouraged, minded, cared for and so on. They want us isolated, weak and powerless. So there are many, many situations in which the narcissistic mothers managed to break up perfectly healthy relationships. But they encourage the toxic ones.

The good news is that once you're aware of this, you can do something about it. The bad news is, it can involve a *lot* of change. More on this later.

We can have difficulty trusting others.

Not surprisingly, DONMs can have difficulty trusting others, especially other women. And often that lack of trust is justified as the tendency, mentioned above, can be to get into relationships with friends and others who are narcissistic or equally toxic.

We can have difficulty showing emotion.

We learned very early that it was not permitted to express emotions. Our 'bad' emotions such as anger or hurt – especially if she was the one causing the anger or hurt – were not allowed. Even if the problem lay elsewhere – a skinned knee, a disappearing boyfriend – she most likely didn't want us annoying her with that. The only way it would be permitted would be if she was feeding off the drama of it, and in that case we didn't feel comfortable expressing those emotions as we knew somehow the response was wrong.

In many cases, too, the narcissistic mothers did not permit us to express happy emotions. Maybe she was threatened by happiness, maybe she resented us getting good feelings from elsewhere through them, who knows … But many DONMs report that if they were expressing joy or happiness their narcissistic mother would make it her business to wipe that smile off their face one way or another.

We can tend to have addictions.

Many DONMs suffer with addictions. And again, this is a logical and appropriate response to the twisted and unbearable conditions in which we find ourselves, and especially to suppressing all our emotions.

And so, DONMs turn to addictions to help with those repressed feelings. And you know, addictions get a bad press, but they do serve a very good and useful purpose. They make the unbearable bearable. They're a sensible solution to a dreadful situation. Every problem was once a solution, and this totally applies to addictions.

The problem with addictions is that they extract such a high price. And so they are not a long-term solution. We need to find better ways to deal with all those emotions, and luckily there is a solution which you can read about on page 155.

We are prone to self-injury and self-neglect.

DONMs not surprisingly can be prone to both proactive self-harm, and self-neglect.

The self-harm is a way of feeling real, of helping the constant pain of being a DONM. It's a way of releasing the pressure of the pain.

As for self-neglect, many of us, especially those with Ignoring Mothers, never learned to look after ourselves. We did learn, however, that we were not worth looking after. And so it can be hard to look after ourselves in adult life. I know that I struggled with this. I did do the necessary, of course, but it took so much energy. I had to fight sabotage nearly every time. It was exhausting. (I sorted it with EFT, as per the script on page 158.)

We can have a disconnect between our thoughts and our feelings.

By this I mean that we don't always know what we feel about a situation. Or even, what we think about it, sometimes. We are so used, so trained, to dismiss our own perceptions that we have to make a special effort to tune into what's going on for us. We have to do consciously what others do without thinking, and like any new skill it takes concentration and energy. This, truly, can be exhausting. I find that even now I have delayed reaction to things. When the situation is happening I don't perceive that something is wrong, but afterwards I replay it and I think, 'Hang on, that was really inappropriate of him / her to say'. At least I do realise it after the event, rather than never realising at all. However, I do wish I could notice it in the moment.

As Jennifer said: 'I realized that my entire life, the way my NM treated me caused a disconnection inside between my feelings and my brain. No wonder I could never recognize when someone was being inappropriate with me, I couldn't figure out my feelings. Now that I'm doing the healing work, I'm learning to reattach my brain to my emotions. Sort of reconnecting the mind-body cord that was severed during my childhood. It is totally like using an unused muscle, and the more we use it, the stronger it gets.'

We can struggle to claim things for ourselves.

Your narcissistic mother no doubt made everything about meeting her needs, as discussed above, and taught you that it was inappropriate for you to look for your needs to be met, or your desires to be honoured.

Here's the thing that we need to remember: being selfish is wanting it to be *inappropriately* about you. But sometimes it really is about you. And that's okay. That's as it should be. That is so important that I'll say it again:

Sometimes it really is about you. And that's okay. That's as it should be.

Your wedding is about you and your spouse-to-be. Not about her. Your university graduation is about you. Your pregnancy is about you. Your new baby is about you and your baby's needs and wishes.

It is not selfish to insist that those things be about you, despite what she tells you.

We can end up either over-achieving, or under-achieving.

Many DONMs either over-achieve, never being able to rest at all, or under-achieve, never reaching their potential.

The over-achievers do so in the never-ending quest to feel good enough, to prove themselves, to finally gain approval. At least they have professional success, but there can be a high personal cost in the feeling of never being good enough and never being able to rest.

Under-achievers can ricochet from financial crisis to financial disaster. Self-sabotage is an element of this. This is related to an inherent feeling of not deserving enough. This makes sense because as the daughter of a narcissistic mother, you were taught that you did not deserve love, or empathy, or validation, or consistency, or even kindness half the time. Material things may have been given to us begrudgingly if at all. So it's understandable that we grow up struggling to believe we deserve good things in life.

Loneliness can be a big issue.

Even if you're in touch with your family, there is a loneliness in being in contact with them. The real you can never connect with them, because they don't want to know the real you, and it's not safe to be vulnerable with them.

Also we can struggle with connecting with others outside the family, for a myriad of reasons. Self-confidence is one, social anxiety is another, lack of good social skills could be yet another.

And there's a kind of existential loneliness, too, if that doesn't sound too flowery. We can struggle with feeling we belong anywhere. After all, if we didn't belong in our own family, where *can* we belong?

We might suffer from social anxiety.

Many DONMs suffer from social anxiety. We have no sense of our place in the world, in our society, our culture. We're not sure how to behave in company. Are we too loud? Too quiet? Too chatty? Not chatty enough? We're always second-guessing ourselves. Add to the fact that, deep down, we all carry a deep shame about who we are, about being born broken as it feels we are, and we might feel that people won't like us. Unfortunately, a lot of the time this can be a self-fulfilling prophesy because people genuinely don't respond well to us. Not because we're not nice, which is what we might think. But because they pick up subliminally on our awkwardness, or discomfort, and react unconsciously to that.

We can have difficulty accepting compliments.

Again not surprisingly, DONMs can have major difficulties accepting compliments. It feels so strange, so *wrong*. The trick is to practise. Just say: 'Thank you, I appreciate you saying that.' That's all. You don't have to comment on the accuracy of the commenter's opinion. But it is courtesy to them to accept their statement and not throw it back in their face.

We are prone to depression.

According to an admittedly unscientific survey on my forum, 90 per cent of DONMs suffer from chronic depression. This is not surprising. We are not allowed to express our feelings, especially our anger, and so they turn inwards, and that can lead to depression.

We can have a history of suicide thoughts and/or attempts.

Many DONMs struggle with suicidal tendencies and/or thoughts, and it would not surprise me if a high percentage of them actually do commit suicide. I know from discussions on the forum that many of us (including me) have a history of suicide attempt(s); we are just the ones who survived them. Again, suicidal feelings make total sense. It is a logical result of feeling so shamed and awful and twisted and broken. Plus it's a logical result of being depressed.

4
THE EMOTIONAL ROLLER-COASTER

Okay, after reading this far you might be reeling with different emotions. Relief is probably a huge one. The knowledge about Narcissistic Personality Disorder explains so very much. It explains *everything*. You're *not* crazy! You were *right* to think things were odd. Your perceptions are right. You are not the flawed person she told you that you were.

And the fact of you being the daughter of a narcissistic mother explains so much about yourself and your negative patterns and your self-sabotage.

There is an elation, a near ecstasy about discovering this. A kind of giddiness. It's like the weight of the world is off your shoulders; there's a freedom from a burden you've been carrying all your life without even knowing it.

Enjoy this feeling. You deserve it. It has been a long, hard, sad, lonely road to this point.

Now you know the truth, and the truth will, indeed, set you free.

But, as Gloria Steinem says, 'The truth will set you free, but first it will piss you off'.

Because there are a lot – a lot – of other emotions to get through once elation has had its play. You are doing no less than entering an absolute roller-coaster of emotions. This list is not exhaustive; nor will the emotions necessarily come in any specific order.

You might experience a huge sense of desolation. Once you realise that your mother has Narcissistic Personality Disorder, and what that entails, then you have to accept, once and for all, that she never loved you. And of course that is a very, very hard thing to accept. We're programmed to want and need our mother's love. Indeed, your whole life up till now might well have been structured around trying to get her love. So the enormity of trying to accept that she never loved you may well leave you struggling and desolate. There's help for this too, in the section on How To Heal on page 129.

Another emotion you might well experience would be grief. This grief could be as strong as if she had died. And in a very real, albeit metaphorical way, she *has* died. Or at least, your image of her, your sense of her, your perception of who she was, has surely died. No wonder you are feeling bereaved.

This *is* a bereavement, make no mistake about that. You have just lost your mother. Well, it's more true to say that you never had her, but it is now that you are accepting that and acknowledging it. So it is now that the bereavement hits. And it's as hard and as devastating as the death of a loving mother would be to another woman. Do not dismiss or underestimate this, truly. You will probably need a period of mourning just as with a death.

But yet, it's worse than that. It's the worst kind of bereavement because it has to be a private one. You must mourn in secret. If a normal woman loses a mother to death, all her family and community rally around and support her. Her job gives her compassionate leave, and understanding if she's a bit slow and weepy for a bit after she comes back. Her friends understand what she's going through and support her.

With your situation, none of that applies. You cannot tell most people that you have just lost your mother. They would not understand and support you. Worse, they will most likely disapprove heartily and let you know it.

There is an EFT script to help you over the bereavement on page 167.

And then, the next stage on the roller-coaster: guilt might rear its head. How could you possibly think so badly of your mother? Your own mother! You are such a horrible and ungrateful daughter.

As part of guilt your thoughts might start playing tricks on you, and no matter how much the awareness of Narcissistic Personality Disorder resonated with you when you heard it first, you might well start second-guessing yourself now. You remind yourself of all the good things she ever did, all the nice things. And you might find yourself minimising the bad things she did to you. It wasn't that bad, you'll think.

This is a good time to introduce the subject of Stockholm Syndrome.

Stockholm Syndrome is, in essence, the trait of abused people to bond closely with their abusers. Another way of describing it is 'trauma bonding'.

It was first identified in 1973 in Stockholm (hence the name) when victims of a bank hostage situation bonded with their hostage-takers to the extent of physically clinging to them to protect them from arrest, and refusing to testify against them in court.

Since then, it has been seen again and again, such as in the cases of Elisabeth Smart, Natascha Kampusch and Jaycee Lee Duggard who all had the opportunity to escape, but didn't take it.

And interestingly, it seems that victims of chronic low-grade abuse can also experience this.

Stockholm Syndrome is a survival trait, and it actually makes sense. If our life is in danger, and the abuser is the one who holds the key, there is a great incentive to form a bond with them.

Now, four distinct situations have to be present in order for Stockholm Syndrome to apply. They are:

- The victim must feel that there is very real danger to their very survival.

- The victim must be cut off from all other perspectives other than those of the abuser – i.e. that the abuser is the only source of information the person receives.
- The victim must have a real, or perceived, inability to escape from the situation.
- The abuser must give occasional kindnesses to the victim.

Now, how do these four elements apply to daughters of narcissistic mothers?

The first definitely applies. As infants and young children our lives truly are in our mother's hands. And if our mother made us feel unsafe, then from our earliest moments our lives felt threatened. Certainly we would not be able to articulate this as such, but we are talking very deep and very primal emotions.

As for the second trait – this is where gaslighting comes in. Our mothers cannot literally and physically isolate us from other perspectives (although many try; many DONMs have had physically isolated upbringings). But they can, and do, psychologically gaslight us, isolating us even from ourselves in a way, and making sure that their perspective is the only one that we believe.

The third trait is of course self-evident. A child does have a very real inabililty to escape from her family. But even more, the abuse can be very subtle (and they tell us it's our fault, etc), so that we don't even realise there's anything to escape from! We are both physically trapped (as children) and emotionally trapped (as children and adults).

And then the fourth trait. The occasional kindnesses. Dutton and Painter, in their 1981 paper on Trauma Bonding, *Emotional Attachments in Abusive Relationships: A Test of Traumatic Bonding Theory*, found that the abuse has to include intermittent kindnesses for this to occur. And there does seem to be a pattern that abusers somehow know this, and do give crumbs of positive reinforcement, or kindnesses. (Consider this: Even Josef Fritzl used to get Christmas trees and other seasonal treats for his cellar children.)

And so, yes, you most likely will feel guilt, huge guilt, at betraying your mother like this, at even *thinking* this badly about her. But remember this: the guilt is *real*, but it is not *true*.

Do you see the distinction?

When you feel the guilt, it is very real. Don't try to deny it or dismiss it or otherwise invalidate or gaslight yourself. It's there. But it is not justified. Guilt is for when we do something wrong. And acknowledging real genuine truth is never wrong.

For now, try not to be fooled by occasional niceness. Healthy relationships are nice the majority of the time. Indeed, I'll go further, and say that while people who are functional and healthy can sometimes be angry, or grumpy, or selfish, or thoughtless etc (same as we all can), they'll never be sneering or nasty or dismissive or cruel.

But even if they are, it should be the absolute exception. Not the normal state of affairs. And there should be a genuine apology and a genuine attempt to stop the dysfunctional behaviour.

So to the next emotion in this roller-coaster.

It might be sadness. Deep, all-pervading sadness. Total grief for that little girl and young woman that you were, who believed all the lies and who wasted so many years trying to please her mother, trying to make herself be good enough to be loved.

And no doubt anger, and even rage, will no doubt rear up too. Fury maybe. How dare she treat you like that? How dare she abuse you? (For abuse is what it was, make no mistake.)

Anger might feel very uncomfortable. Again, that's not surprising. You probably were not allowed to express, or to even feel, anger, before now. So this anger might feel threatening and, as I say, uncomfortable.

Along with the anger you might have very vivid dreams or fantasies of inflicting violence on her. You might shock yourself at how detailed and violent those fantasies are.

Again, these fantasies are normal – many DONMs get them. And despite what your narcissistic mother taught you, all feelings are appropriate. To me, these fantasies are the long-buried anger coming out. And they're empowering – you have felt so scared of her for so long, and now your subconscious is discovering its strength.

Needless to say, inflicting real violence on her would be totally wrong, both legally and morally.

But fantasies do no harm, and they seem to be a process to go through, and will ease after a while. EFT can help to move them on too.

You might feel some more guilt then, at your feelings of violence. But the same applies to that guilt as to the original guilt: allow it, don't deny it. But don't believe it.

Another emotion might well be fear for the future – what now, for your relationship with her? How will you relate to her now? There's more information about that coming up on page 78.

If you're Christian you might butt up against the issue about honouring your mother and father. Is thinking this about your mother dishonouring her? (A very good website for Christians with toxic parents is http://www.luke173ministries.org/)

And then another twist in the roller-coaster … hope might raise its head.

Maybe you're wrong about all of this!

Maybe if you try just a tiny bit harder, you can sort it out with her, earn her love, get a proper relationship with her. This is, of course, back to The Big Lie. But that lie is entrenched. Of course it is going to surface again.

This is very tempting. Very tempting indeed. It's human nature to want to think that we can fix things. To accept that this situation is unfixable is to accept that you are powerless over it, that there is nothing that you can do. I repeat: when you're dealing with NPD, there *is* nothing you can do to fix things. And although accepting that is hard, with that acceptance comes peace.

Or, you might consider this: perhaps you can explain to her about NPD and then she'll understand what has been wrong all these years, and you can start creating a good and healthy relationship with each other. There is information beginning on page 78 on how to relate to your mother now that you have this information, but for now can I just suggest that you *not* do this until you have read the rest of this book. Just park the hope for now. (I know, I know: the car park is getting full at this stage!)

Despair is another ingredient in this roller-coaster. How can you possibly heal from all the fallout of this? How can you ever reclaim all the things that should have been your birthright, such as self-esteem and confidence? We'll talk more about this too.

But yet, there's a kind of hope as well. Maybe you *can* heal! Now that you know so much was not true ... it's all to play for now, isn't it? There's more information about that later on in this book too.

It can all take a while to process.

The other thing to remember is that what I call the N-realisation is overwhelming. It's huge. It's massive. Don't underestimate the enormity of this. You have, after a lifetime of lies, realised the truth. You will find that you re-evaluate everything. Memories will pop up by themselves, like little bubbles, and you'll look at them with your new awareness, and you'll be able to say, with an overwhelming rush of recognition, 'So *that's* what was going on there! It all makes sense now. NPD is why she was so excited when I miscarried my baby / was sulky when I won that award / was mean to my new partner!!'

This is a wonderful experience, as you see the events of your life as they really were, without the N-filters she put on you.

But, as wonderful as this is, it's exhausting. And it can seem endless. Sometimes the memories that come up, pressing for attention to be re-evaluated, can seem overwhelming.

The good news is that it is finite. It might seem endless, but it is not. Just go with it for now. The rush of memories will ease off in time.

But processing it all, and coming to terms with it all, is still massive work. Don't underestimate it. Give yourself the space and time to deal with it. I remember I took about three months doing little more than processing this. It was a life-changing shock. Yes, change for the better. But still a shock.

And so, to deal with all of this, I suggest the following:

Take deep breaths. Literally. Every time you feel yourself getting overwhelmed or stressed by this, consciously take at least ten deep breaths. When we're stressed we breathe from our chest, and physically doing the opposite of that, i.e. breathing from our diaphragm, calms us.

Try EFT. See page 143 for more on this.

Know that this will pass. It's a process, not a situation. You're not doomed to live in this chaos and confusion forever.

Accept the confusion. Don't try to fight it. You are processing huge stuff here. You're changing your very paradigm, or world-view, of how life is, and who *you* are. That's massive work all by itself – of course it's going to cause upheaval. So don't try to fight that.

If at all possible don't do any other big life-change stuff while this process is going on, say for three months or so. So if you can avoid moving house, changing jobs, etc, then do so. You don't need more stress right now.

Accept all the feelings. Don't berate yourself for having them. They are what they are, just accept them. (This is also good practice in changing the rules she gave you. She told you what to feel and what not to feel. Here, you are giving yourself permission to feel whatever you feel.) Try to observe the feelings if possible – that stops them being so overwhelming. Observe them and accept them without swimming in them. This technique can take practice, but it's very much worth doing.

If you have a partner, ask him / her to support you during this time. They don't have to understand what's going on on, and indeed they will probably struggle to understand, just to accept and support you. The same goes for adult children. If you have younger children then it's not appropriate to burden them with this, just try to put on a brave face for them as much as possible.

Be kind to yourself. Give yourself little treats such as a nice walk, a hot bath, a couple of hours to read a novel and so on. Being nice to yourself might seem very challenging and just *wrong*, so don't do it if it causes more stress. But if at all possible, nurture yourself at this time.

Acknowledge, applaud and maybe even celebrate your courage. You're facing up to something most people can never bring themselves to do, i.e. the fact that your mother was abusive. Be proud of that.

One big issue you'll have to deal with, while on this roller-coaster, is, what now for your relationship with her? That's what we talk about next.

5
YOUR FUTURE RELATIONSHIP WITH HER

Now that you know all this you might be tempted to tell her that you think she's narcissistic. There are two possible reasons why you might want to do this.

The first is a very real and understandable need/desire to throw it in her face. 'Ha!' you want to say, 'It wasn't me at all, the way you said it was. It was *you* all along!'

Another reason might be that part of you hopes that when you explain about NPD, slowly and in words of one syllable, she'll *finally* get it! She'll understand what's been wrong with your relationship and will change and all will end happily.

Well ... no.

The thing about narcissists, as we have been discussing, is that they believe they're perfect, they *need* to believe they're perfect, and they will never even consider that they are in any way less than perfect.

So she will categorically not be able to hear you say that she has a personality disorder. Interestingly, some narcissistic mothers have recognised it in others around them, other family members, maybe. But they'll never recognise it in themselves.

In fact, she will feel extremely attacked, threatened and under siege if you dare suggest she's less than perfect. This makes sense – if their whole being depends on them being perfect, then you genuinely are attacking that by suggesting otherwise.

Let me explain it this way. Your whole being, your whole existence, depends on you getting sufficient air, right? So if someone tried to deprive you of that, then you'd (rightly) feel threatened, attacked, and under siege, wouldn't you?

And more, you'd do whatever it took to remove that threat and regain your needed air. That would become your ultimate goal, and nothing else – *nothing else* – would matter until you had regained your supply of air.

You wouldn't care what you had to do, what violence you had to inflict, in order to get air into your lungs. Your very survival would be at stake and nothing else would matter.

That is an exact analogy for what a narcissist experiences when you dare to suggest she's less than perfect. I know it's hard for us to get our heads around, but for her, her supposed perfection is as essential to her survival as air is to you and me.

So, the answer is, don't tell her about your NPD discovery.

Well, do if you want! It's not my place to tell you what to do and this book is about empowering you, and me telling you what to do would be disempowering you.But do know that it will not do any good to tell her, and that you will be subjecting yourself to gaslighting, invalidation, and Narcissistic Rage if you do.

So what do you do?

So, what do you do next, now that you know the truth? There are two parallel avenues here. The first is your own healing from the lies and the dysfunction and the abuse. We explore that beginning on page 129.

The second is, how are you going to deal with your mother now?

You have three options:

1. Carry on as you always have, but with your new awareness protecting you.
2. Begin to enact a situation that's called Low Contact, or LC.
3. Cut her off entirely, which is called No Contact, or NC.

More on those in a minute. But first: There's another option, kinda, which is one that a number of DONMs take, and that is to suggest to their narcissistic mother that she and they go to counselling together. Your mother might even agree to that. But her motivation will be to get *you* fixed, so that you get back to being her biddable daughter. If you do that, make sure that *you* pick the therapist as per the information on page 139. I do not expect that the counselling will work to get you and your mother to a workable relationship, but it still can be worth it for letting you know that you have done all possible to repair the relationship.

As you read through these options bear in mind that there is no right or wrong except what is right or wrong for *you*. I do not advocate any particular option, nor am I trying to guide you to any specific decision. I lay out the options and it is for you to decide what is right for you.

So, the first option in dealing with your mother is to carry on seeing her as often as you already have, but keeping your new awareness in mind. Now that you know what's going on, you can try not to take her narcissistic games personally. Because in truth, they're *not* personal. For a narcissist, as we know, nothing is about you; everything is about her. So her games and rages and upset are all about her. Make that trait work for you instead of against you as it has your whole life, and here are a few suggestions on how to do that:

One trick is to pretend that you are a scientist or anthropologist studying a strange culture. So when she does her narcissistic stuff, just observe it as dispassionately as you can. Maybe even try to be somewhat amused by it, at the predictability of it all. You can play mental Narcissism Bingo:

Narcissistic Rage	Narcissistic Huff	Narcissistic Glow	Trumping your stories
Self-praise	Talking over you	Gaslighting	Favouritism
Playing victim	Provoking drama	Pseudo-sympathy for others' tragedies	Fauxpology
Tears	Put-downs	Martyr: 'Don't mind me'	Blame-shifting

Or pretend you are all in a play, and her part is the narcissistic mother (and, oh boy, but she plays it so well. A natural ...), and you are the daughter who is patient with that, but well able to rise above it without being affected by it, and perhaps even be amused by it. You might even throw her little bones: 'Oh this cake you baked is *so* good, Mum', and watch her quiver with narcissistic glow.

You might choose to stop giving her hostages to fortune. In other words, don't share your upsets and worries with her – she'll only suck them up and feed off them, and will not be any support to you whatsoever. Similarly, don't share your successes with her either, as she will dismiss and diminish them to your face, and then crow about them to her acquaintances. Try not to share your celebratory occasions with her either, so that she does not get to spoil them.

I consider this option to be a *weather–topic relationship*. In other words, you talk only about the weather and other topics of such little interest. And her. Talk about her. Or rather, let her talk about her. On the rare occasions my mother asked about me after I initiated this weather-topic relationship, she was very (pathetically, hilariously) easily deflected back into talking about herself. It was exactly like diverting a toddler!

I did this for a number of years and it worked really well. It was horrible for me, of course, because there was no authenticity in it, and no connection. It was, in some ways, a denial of my very Self. But it protected that same Self from her abuse, and was a workable solution.

Superficial relationships can work very well with a narcissist. For a certain value of 'very well', that is. You won't get any satisfaction or support or friendship or any good thing from it. But you'll still be in touch with your mother, and it'll be mostly bearable.

She might pick up that things have changed. You're not giving her any drama fodder after all. She might complain about this. 'You've changed', she might say petulantly. 'You don't tell me anything any more.'

And you deflect it lightly, 'But didn't I tell you about my trip to the hairdressers just now? Oh and speaking of which, did you get *your* hair done? It looks lovely!'

She might try and pick at various scabs: 'What happened with that row you were having with the car dealership?'

'Oh that got resolved', you say, even if it hasn't, 'they paid up.'

She might try to provoke you, to get some drama, some Narcissistic Supply. 'Have you put on weight?' she'll ask.

'Very possibly,' you answer lightly. Always choose the answer that agrees with her, as it cuts off the drama supply. And try distraction again, 'Oh look at the lovely daffodils out there!'

She might persist, ignoring the daffodils, 'Yes, I was thinking you're looking a bit fat. You'll need to watch it.'

'I surely will. It's early for daffodils, isn't it? But they look well.'

And so on and so on. This takes practice, and it can be hard not to be sucked in. But there is a lot of satisfaction in seeing her thwarted and frustrated, and all by you being polite and pleasant.

In this way, one by one, you cut the drama-threads and leave only bland innocuous marshmallows of conversation.

Low Contact

The second option is to Low Contact or LC. A lot of DONMs choose this one because they find that their mother drains them of all their energy when they meet her, and they no longer want to inflict that on themselves. Or at least, they want to limit their exposure to that.

There are two ways to go LC. One is to just do it, and the other is to announce it. They both have their pros and cons, and which one you choose will probably depend on whether she's an Engulfing mother or an Ignoring mother.

If she's an Ignoring mother, you can just cut down on how often you see her, and she probably won't even notice. The fact she doesn't notice can actually hurt quite a bit, which might be counter-intuitive. You *want* to cut down contact, and you have, and now you're not happy that that's what happened ... maybe she was right all along that there is no pleasing you.

But here's the thing. You don't *want* to cut down contact. You want the contact to be healthy and wholesome and good. You want your mother, and nothing changes that. When you go LC, it's because you have to, not because you want to.

And if she accepts it without querying it or without even noticing, of course that hurts. It's proof positive that you meant nothing to her. It does hurt. I know that. I suggest the EFT script on page 170 to help erase this pain.

Now, if she's an Engulfing mother then it works slightly differently. If you just try to ease off on how often you see her, she'll notice immediately and resist that with all her might. So you will need to formally advise her of this. She will not like it of course, and will resist. Read up on the information on setting boundaries on page 85 for more on how to manage her resistance.

What you can do is to tell her formally how often you will see her. You can give her a reason, or not, as you choose. But a good rule of thumb with narcissists is to choose the option that has the least potential for drama. And if you give her a reason she can argue it and gaslight you around it and so on.

I suggest giving her the LC information in writing, by letter or e-mail, rather than verbally, so that she cannot confuse you or distract your or divert you.

So here is a suggested LC letter. Note the diplomatic lie in it – just something to soften the blow for her.

Dear Mum,

I am writing to advise you that I will not be able to visit you three times a week as I have been doing up till now. From now on we will only be able to visit once a week – either me to your house, or yours to mine. Also you will need to phone before coming over to my house as I'm not in a position to have you just drop in any longer. Also, I will only be able to speak with you on the phone a maximum of once a day, and for a maximum of fifteen minutes each time.

It will be nice to see you and talk to you when we do, and I look forward to that.

All best,

Now, she might well react in a number of ways.

One possible reaction is that she will just ignore the letter and carry on as before, calling three times a day, or just dropping into the house as before.

Or she might phone you, or call around, in a narcissistic rage and demand to know what you're thinking of to be so unreasonable, and how *dare* you refuse to take her calls/bar her from your house.

Or she might play the victim. Send you an email back, or phone, sobbing that she doesn't know what she has done to deserve this cruel, *cruel* treatment from you, that she has always done her best as your mother, and loves you so much, etc, etc.

If her other tricks don't work, she might send an emissary known as a Flying Monkey to plead her case. Your father, or step-father, is a good bet for this role, but really anyone will do once they'll take her side. This Flying Monkey will tell you something like, 'Your mother's so upset you know. I'm really worried for her health. She had a panic attack when she got your letter. We nearly had to call an ambulance. You know her heart isn't good'. There's more about Flying Monkeys on page 100)

Keeping to boundaries

Here is how keeping to boundaries works. You need to decide on a consequence for every boundary. Leaving her company (if you're with her) or hanging up (if you're on the phone) are good ones. Asking her to leave if she's in your house, but having a plan for if she doesn't leave, such as going upstairs and locking yourself in your bedroom. The consequence must always be something that is in *your* control to enact.

So the steps are as follows:

- Set the boundary. You can do this in the moment: 'Mum, I'm asking you to stop bad-mouthing Gerry', or ahead of time, 'Mum, I need you to stop bad-mouthing my siblings to me'.
- If it continues, you say it again, a bit more firmly: 'Mum, I really am asking you to stop bad-mouthing Gerry to me. You need to stop doing that.' Or, if you're reminding her of a pre-set boundary, 'Mum, remember I asked you to stop bad-mouthing my siblings to me? Well you're bad-mouthing Gerry now and you need to stop.'
- If she continues, you threaten the consequence: 'Mum, if you don't stop, I am leaving / hanging up.'

- If she continues, you say, 'I told you I would have to leave/hang up if you didn't stop. You didn't stop, so I need to go/hang up. Goodbye.' And – this is the essential bit – you carry out the consequence, calmly and firmly with no further discussion. If she asks why you're leaving you can repeat, 'I told you I would leave if you didn't stop. You didn't stop, so I am leaving'. But you do *not* get into an argument or discussion about it – that is essential. You let nothing at all stop you from carrying out the consequence. No apologies, no tears, no appeals. She has to learn. Remember that she's a toddler in a grown woman's body. Toddlers (and puppies, think of training puppies) learn by enforcing consequences.
- And repeat the next time. And the time after that. It might well take several episodes of you carrying out the consequence for her to understand that you mean it. And she will probably never stop trying to push the boundaries. She might sneak in a tiny, mild, criticism of Gerry, maybe, looking at you slyly to see how you react. And if you let that one go, she'll come in with a slightly worse one. Pushing her luck, in other words. You will have to be very clear on how tightly you enforce the boundaries, and then do that. This is *exhausting.* There is no denying that. But you have no options other than to do it, or to go back to how you were.

She will resist the boundaries another way too, by complaining about them. She might say (tearfully, or crossly), things like, "You've changed! You're always angry. Why can't you be the lovely daughter you used to be". It can be hard to resist this, but remember she's just a toddler protesting about not getting her own way.

You can respond to these statements in the same light way recommended above, ignoring the wobbly lip or the snarl she might be showing. 'I haven't changed a bit, Mum. Oh, look at the lovely daffodils'.

LC is hard to maintain. Going to see her that once-weekly (or however often you've decided upon) is still hard. It opens the wounds each time. She'll no doubt get a dig in every time. You are constantly manning the boundaries. It's not easy. But then, nothing with a narcissistic mother is easy. They are masters at creating no-win situations.

One thing to remember, however, is this mantra:

'If one of us has to be upset, it doesn't have to be me.'

Now, of course, in an ideal world, populated with healthy people, we would work on the situation and come up with a win-win solution in which neither of us is upset.

But as you well know, that ideal situation does not ever apply when we're dealing with narcissists. Or even other dysfunctional people.

And so a situation is created in which one of you *does* have to be upset. Either she gets her way and then *you'll* be upset. Or you get your way and then *she'll* be upset.

So, this is a situation in which the first half of the mantra applies, i.e. that one of you has to be upset.

But ... it doesn't have to be you!

This is revolutionary. At least, it was for me when I first realised it. You mean, I could just let *her* be upset at not getting her own way?

For sure, I didn't want her upset. It wasn't nice when she was upset. But at the end of the day, I still had a choice. Either she could be upset, or I could. And it didn't have to be me. Especially since she was the one creating the situation in which one of us had to be upset. If it were up to me I'd go for the win-win situation every time. Not my fault that wasn't possible.

Now, it's possible that you will feel an inordinate fear of her, and be terrified of upsetting her her. Totally natural, given your upbringing. But you can erase that fear, and see her posturing as just the tantrums of a toddler. (This of course, does not apply if she's genuinely violent or otherwise dangerous. But if she is those things, she probably isn't narcissistic alone.)

You can use EFT to erase this fear, and the script on page 174 will help you and allow you to do that.

And remember, if one of you has to be upset, it doesn't have to be you!

Going No Contact

Going No Contact, or NC, is a big decision. Be in no doubt about that. It means to cut off all contact with your narcissistic mother, and possibly other family members too, by default, as we shall explore later.

This is such a big, complex, difficult step. Many DONMs genuinely do love their mothers, and it seems impossible to cut those ties. And even for those of us, like me, who never ever loved her, it's still a huge step. Everything in our culture *screams* at us that you must stay in contact with your mother. It's ironic because no one nowadays would ever tell you to stay with an abusive spouse (and it's hard to remember, but they used to), but they all tell you to stay with these parents. Especially since the abuse is so subtle, it's even more difficult to explain.

Remember I spoke earlier of how there are three layers of abuse to this NPD? The first layer is our mother's abuse. The second layer is her denial of it and invalidation of our experiences. The third layer is *society's* denial of it, and invalidation of our experiences.

And if you go No Contact, it's very possible that others – neighbours, friends, extended family – will judge you harshly for it. This can be difficult to deal with. As Lucinda on the forum said, 'I struggled with this because I thought their opinions of me somehow defined who I really was. If they thought I was bad it felt like I really was bad.'

She then realised, however, 'When I got to know myself I realized I'm fine just the way I am. I know I'm a good person. Other people's opinions are just their opinions, they are not who I am.'

Sometimes DONMs find themselves hoping for their narcissistic mother to do something really big and awful, just one more thing, to justify going No Contact. Again, this is a very valid position to hold, but I do offer you the opportunity of considering all the awful things she has done already. Do you *really* need her to do one more thing? Try the writing exercise on page 133 to answer that question.

Just like with an abusive spouse, sometimes we have to go back to the abuse of our mother time and again until finally we reach the place of being able to say, *Enough.* And that's okay, you know. There's no one standing there with a stopwatch or an impatiently tapping foot. You don't have to prove yourself to anyone else. You will do what you do, when you do it, and that's okay.

Or sometimes DONMs feel somehow as if they need permission to go No Contact. Someone to tell them it's okay. Well, in truth you don't need anyone's permission. But just in case, I give you mine:

I tell you categorically that no one has to stay with an abuser. No one is obliged to endure being psychologically and emotionally invalidated, lied to, lied about, undermined, dismissed and otherwise mistreated. I tell you that you have every right to only associate with people who treat you well and considerately. And that being biologically related to your abuser does not change that one bit.

You might think that it's not fair to punish her. Thing is, you're *not* punishing her. You're protecting yourself by removing yourself from an abuser. If she does not like it, that is just a consequence. It's a subtle distinction but a real one. You are not doing it *to* her, you are doing it *for you*, and any impact on her is the consequence of that. Indeed, another meaning of the initials NC is Natural Consequences. She is experiencing the natural consequences of her actions, and it is not your job to protect her from those.

But she can't help what she does, you might think next. True, in a way. She *can* act differently, but her NPD wouldn't let her, so yes, she can't help it. That still does not mean we have to put up with that treatment.

Put it this way: I know that a tiger cannot help being the way she is. I know that a tiger is a natural predator and will kill me given the chance. I do not blame her for that – she cannot help it. But I make it my business not to go near tigers, for my own safety. No blame whatsoever. Just avoidance. (We speak more about this topic on page 135 when we discuss forgiveness.)

So NC is not something you do *to* her. It's something you do *for* you, for your health and sanity and well-being.

Now, let's be very clear. NC has a very specific meaning. It means *no* contact. Just like you can't be a little bit pregnant, you can't be a little bit No Contact. You either are, or you are not. If you have any contact at all, you are LC. Which is a perfectly legitimate thing to be. It's just not NC.

This fact that No Contact means exactly that: no contact, is *descriptive* not *prescriptive.* By which I mean, this is not me, or anyone else telling you what to do. That always remains your choice. Your narcissistic mother tried to limit your choices and options. This book and what I share in it do exactly the opposite. They are about empowering you and describing your choices and options, with no agenda as to which ones you pick.

No Contact means:

- You do not speak to her. Ever. No matter what. She is dead to you, in effect.
- You do not listen to her, or give her another chance, or hear her out. You tried that. It did not work, remember? It *will not* work because your mother is a narcissist and narcissists do not change.
- You do not let her into your house.
- You do not go to her house.
- You do not phone her. You do not answer her phone calls. Screen your calls if possible. If you answer the phone and it is her, hang up immediately without giving her any response.
- Do not send or answer her e-mails or other correspondence. Do not even read them. They will be full of lies which will upset you. Block her emails if possible. (Keep her correspondence in a file

though, as proof if you need to apply for a restraining order, of which more below.)

- If possible, do not accept gifts in the post from her. If those gifts arrive, then just donate them to a charity shop. Do not send them back as that is more Narcissistic Supply. Do not send thank-you letters. I know that feels rude, but it is not. The normal rules do not apply with narcissists, as she is using those gifts to manipulate. If you have to sign for the parcels, don't – just refuse them.
- If you need to communicate, say if you have a business or property in common, do so through solicitors.
- Do not send her cards. No, not even for her birthday, or Mother's Day, or Christmas.
- Unfriend her on Facebook. Block her too, so she can't see your statuses.
- Nothing trumps NC. So no matter how big the news or the event, you do not involve them. So your wedding, the birth of your children, the weddings of your children will all happen without her. Yes, this is very, very sad. Yes, it is very, very necessary. Remember how she spoiled all the special occasions you *did* let her get involved in.
- If you meet her in public, ignore her if possible. If that would cause upset and grief for others (say at a party or function you are at), then do the bare minimum you can possibly get away with. Do not let her use this opportunity to try to suck you into discussion.
- Do not discuss her with others who are in contact with her. This is very important as she will probably send them to argue her case. More on this below.

I strongly advise that you think about what you will do in various scenarios that she might try. It's essential to have a plan so you are not taken by surprise when it happens. It's hard to think strategically when we are stressed.

So, if she comes to the front door of your house and knocks on it, how will you react? If you are NC, you do not answer the door – but what will you do? Retreat upstairs? Go to the kitchen?

Or, if you open the door by mistake, what will you do? Again, for NC, the only appropriate reaction is to close the door in her face. (I know this seems extreme. But see page 97 for information about how normal rules don't apply with narcissists). If you answer the phone and it's her, what will you do? Speak to her? Hang up? Put the phone down without hanging up and walk away?

Now, this is very important – not only do you need to plan all this, but I strongly advise you to practise it too. There is a reason actors rehearse so extensively; sportspeople practise so much. It's because the body needs to know what to do without thinking. It needs to know its role by habit, without having to consciously do it. When you are under stress, you tend to revert to known actions, and closing doors on your mother, or hanging up on her, are not known actions. Not until you make them so, anyway, which is the point.

So, silly though it might feel, rehearse this. If at all possible get someone to take the role of your mother, banging on the door, plaintively calling you through the letterbox, for example.

It might sound excessive to do all this, but it will bring you peace. You won't have to wonder what you'll do in any given situation, you'll *know*! And you'll have rehearsed it. You will be prepared, so you no longer have to fret about it but can go about your life.

All this is important because No Contact is THE END. You have already done everything possible to try to create a good healthy relationship and it has not worked.

There is nothing left for you to try. It is time for you to walk away, to concentrate on your healing (of which more below) and to create your own life in your own way, to create the life you deserve. It is time for you to put your energy into finding and creating healthy mutually-empowering relationships and not to waste time banging on a door that will never open.

No Contact will give you peace and tranquillity such as you cannot imagine right now. It will free you from living in the web of lies she created. It will free you from trying to be this mythical perfect person she demanded you try to be (and then made sure you could not be).

Now, having said all that, you can break No Contact at any time. You have the absolute right to do that. This is about meeting *your* needs, and sometimes you need to try again, to double check if she was as bad as you thought.

You might fall for her tricks and get sucked back in. That's okay. Don't beat yourself up over it. You get as many chances as you need to get this right. And even that word, 'right', only means, 'right for you'. There is no arbiter, no judge. This is about empowering *you* and meeting *your* needs.

So, now that you know what No Contact means, how do you do it?

You either just stop contacting her and wait for her to get the hint, ignoring all contact in the meantime, or you write a No Contact letter. Again, it is up to you what you do, but I do recommend the No Contact letter as it will make it mentally easier for you to ignore her attempts at contacting you if you have already told her why.

So, what do you put in a No Contact letter? I strongly suggest that you put as absolutely little as possible. I know it is tempting to pour your heart onto the page, and tell her exactly what has been wrong with your relationship all these years, and why you're cutting her off – but this can backfire hugely. That will just give her ammunition to come back and gaslight you with ('That *never* happened!') and to smear you with in the inevitable smear campaign.

I know there might be a residual hope that if you pour your heart out and show her that you're so upset about these events, and so serious about them that you are going to cut off contact, it will make her realise her mistakes. It won't. It really, really will not. She is a narcissist. She cannot accept responsibility for her actions. She cannot accept that she has done anything wrong.

Now, it absolutely *is* a good idea to write that heart-felt letter, pouring it all out. Just don't send it. Write it for *you*. Write it to remind yourself of all that she did, so you can refer to it if you are tempted to contact her again (and your mind will play those tricks on you, which we discuss more below). Write it so that you can claim your right to speak your truth despite the lies she forced on you.

Or, if you do write it to send, make sure you are sending it for your own reasons. For the satisfaction of finally having spoken your truth. Don't send it hoping it'll make her have a change of heart, because, as already said, that will not happen.

Here's one suggestion for an NC letter, based on the one I myself wrote.

Dear ...

I have realised that our relationship is intrinsically dysfunctional, toxic and emotionally abusive, and that I will be far healthier and happier if I remove myself from it. Therefore I ask you not to contact me again. I do not do this in anger, or offence, but rather in profound sadness. But I do ask it. Any further communication from you will be binned unopened/deleted unread. Despite everything, I wish you all the best for your future.

Note that I included the best wishes for the future because I was careful not to go NC in anger or revenge.

You may choose to send the NC letter registered post so that she cannot deny having received it.

So, what will happen when she receives your NC letter?

Possibly nothing. It is very possible that she will not react at all, that you will never hear from her again. If she is an Ignoring NM that is more likely.

In one way it is a relief not to hear from her. You wanted NC, and you have it.

But yet, it hurts. It hurts that she dropped you so easily. That you meant so little to her. It's a real slap in the face. You can use the EFT script on page 170 to erase this hurt. But also, remember that if it were different and she had hounded you, it's not because she loved you. It would be because she didn't want to lose her chew toy, frankly. She didn't want to lose the source of Narcissistic Supply.

And so, if she does not do anything, you are off the hook. Free to do the emotional work of healing and start creating your own best life. You can go straight to page 129 to see how to do just that. And if she does contact you at a later stage, you can come back here to read about that.

However ...

It is equally likely that she will do some, or all, of a number of things. Note that if you are genuinely NC, you won't know about any of these. You'll have built a wall that her attempts cannot cross, and that will save you a *lot* of pain and upset. Here is what she'll try anyway:

She might start what's called *hoovering*. Which is as the name suggests – an attempt to suck you up again. This involves hounding you. Stalking you even. Demanding that you tell her what she's done wrong. Or imploring piteously. Crying maybe. Whatever it takes.

I might sound hard and cynical. That's because I am. I have read too many experiences of DONMs on my forum to have any remaining illusions about how sincere these women are.

So if temper will work, she'll do that. If demands might work, she'll try those. If neither of those work she'll try tears. As I said, whatever it takes. When those things don't work, she'll up the ante. You may get a call that she's in hospital. Has been diagnosed with a terminal illness. The roof has fallen off her house ... Of course, if you do get in touch, you'll find that that message was very much exaggerated. The terminal illness diagnosis? She was in hospital for minor tests.

She might send you a letter full of what, at first glance, seems like remorse and apologies. But when you look at it analytically you'll see the narcissistic tricks running through it. Sarah from our forum wrote a template letter for the narcissistic mothers (or in her case, her narcissistic mother-in-law), which I share here with her permission:

Dear [make sure you include insincere expressions of affection from the beginning to encourage a false sense of security and hope that this will be a nice letter] <insert name>,

I understand that you think I have done something wrong. [It is VITAL that you word this very carefully, as the recipient of the letter needs to assume you are expressing you have heard their concerns, but you need to ensure you are actually blaming them for their interpretation of the situation.] I am very sorry that you think I hurt you. [Again, wording here is VITAL – you can now tell anyone who will listen that you have made an apology, when acceptance of the apology would actually mean the victim accepting responsibility.]

I feel that you have misunderstood me and I'm extremely hurt that you would think these things about me. You need to understand that everything I do is out of love, and all I know how to do is love. [Do not underestimate the importance of these 2 messages – you need to turn things around so that you are the hurt victim. The follow-up sentence is a brilliant way to avoid responsibility for any of your actions. It also confuses the victim – how can they think you have been mean when you are such a loving person?]

I had no idea you felt so mistreated. [This puts responsibility on the victim again – how were you meant to care about their feelings if you didn't know those feelings existed? Make sure you use a strong word like mistreated as it makes the victim feel they have gone too far in their objections to your behaviour.]

[Now it's time to get a little creative. Include at least 3 examples of incidents that happened and go to town invalidating the victim's reality of those events. Remember to use specific quotes that didn't actually happen, and make sure at least one example quotes the victim being nasty to you (make this up).]

I never...

I was hurt that you think I ...

Do you remember that you ...

[name of friend/relative]and [name of friend/relative] have both told me they have also been shocked and hurt by your behaviour and they can't believe you are treating me this way. [The victim must feel isolated and slightly crazy that others believe you are right.]

I am hoping that you will do the right thing and make the family whole again. [This is optional, but useful as a guilt tool to make the victim responsible for the happiness of the entire family now that you have firmly established that the relationship problems are her fault.]

Love from your ever loving [undermine their feelings that this letter is nasty] MUM [If you can use caps for MUM that will reinforce your status in their life.]

Another hoovering attempt is that she might send a card. Mandy on the forum received a card. She fretted over it, saying, 'The ball is back in my court now. It'd be rude not to respond. And they'd see my lack of response as more evidence of how rude I am.'

The fact is that the ball is *not* back in her court, or yours. It would *not* be rude to not respond. This card is not genuine; it's manipulation, and it's not rude to ignore attempts at manipulation.

One of the biggest weapons that narcissists use against us is our manners. They put us in no-win situations where our niceness and our decency and our social awareness trap us.

But, with narcissists, the normal rules don't apply. That might seem quite radical, but it's really good news. *They* break all the rules of social interaction and human co-operation, and therefore we are not bound to those rules either when we're dealing with them. And as they are not playing by the rules of society, then *you* are at a serious disadvantage if you do keep playing by those rules.

Which is, of course, what they are counting on.

I know it goes against the grain to throw out the normal rules, and can seem shocking to do, but once you get the hang of it, it is very liberating.

So, you don't have to thank them for gifts or cards (such 'gifts' really just being drama-fodder and manipulation anyway, as we said.).

You don't have to send them birthday or other cards.

You don't have to include them in your family celebrations.

You don't have to return their phone calls, texts, or emails.

You don't have to 'friend' them on Facebook, or respond to their statuses if they are a friend.

With narcissists, normal rules don't apply. They just don't.

The only rule that you need to worry about is the rule to protect yourself and your family from her manipulation.

So I suggest you watch out for the times she tries to manipulate you into doing things because it's the polite thing to do ... and refuse to fall for it.

The great news is that you have way more power than you realise, you truly do. And that power is to ignore. It's like kryptonite to narcissists. Works on them every time. And for bonus goodness and satisfaction, they *hate* it. Not that I recommend doing anything petty and nasty to them, but if you do something for your own well-being and it upsets them, well, I think there's no harm in taking pleasure in that. It's little enough after all we've been put through.

So, the motto is DAI: *Delete And Ignore.*

For sure, they will take your lack of response as more evidence for whatever they believe about you. Thing is, they believe these things anyway. If you respond to the card they're not going to suddenly think, 'Oh she's so good, so genuine, we can start treating her well'.

At a very deep level your freedom lies in not caring what they think. Or caring, if you must, but not letting it influence the actions you take in pursuing your own health and well-being. Which, let me stress, are *far* more your responsibility than is pandering to your mother's games.

Another trick she might try is to contact you and offer to meet to discuss it all. This is very tempting – after all, your dearest wish is to have a proper relationship with her, and here she is opening the door to that. How can you possibly refuse?

Well, you may recall that you tried everything before going NC. That you were driven to it by years and years of trying to discuss it, to no avail. You may decide that there is nothing to be gained by this.

But more likely you'll think that you owe it to her, to yourself, and/or to your relationship, to give it every chance. Which is a totally valid position to hold.

But meeting her probably will be a very bad idea. She will just gaslight, invalidate, twist, spin facts, etc, etc, as she always did.

I strongly suggest, instead, that you ask her to write out – in detail – what she plans to say, and send it to you, telling her that you will then decide if it's worth meeting in person.

Her reaction to this request will tell you a lot. Most likely she will be furious at you demanding this, and will refuse to do it. Or she might agree to do it, and then not. If she agrees to do it, then leave the ball in her court. Don't chase her for it.

If a letter comes back saying something like: 'I want to discuss how we can sort this out and become friends again', that's too vague. Write back to her (if you want) saying that you need to hear the details of how she proposes to sort it out.

If you do meet with her, either with, or without, her written submission, then meet in a public place that you can leave as you choose. And for choice, bring an advocate with you, as support and witness.

Another form of hoovering is to send you an apology. A fauxpology most likely, but cunningly disguised as real. Remember the rules of real apologies shared on page 35, and check her apology against that.

With all this hoovering you might well get sucked in and go back to her. It's easily done, especially since we so desperately want to believe our mothers.

Most likely she'll be nice for a while if you do that. And so you will feel loads of guilt for having doubted her and rejected her, along with relief that you're all getting on so well, and hopes for an amicable future.

It won't last though. Once she has you properly reeled back in, she will revert to her original self. Or even – very possibly – she will be nastier than her normal self, to punish you for having dared to reject her. This vicious turnaround can leave you reeling.

Another trick she might try is to send others to argue her case – people called Flying Monkeys, after the creatures in *The Wizard Of Oz*. 'Fly my pretties, fly' – those ones. This could be her husband / your father, a sibling, an aunt. It will be someone well used to the enabling role.

The Flying Monkey might agree with you when you speak of what she has done, but ask you to accept her bad behaviour anyway: 'I know she's hard to get on with, I do really. But that's just her way. She can't help it. You know how she is. Can you not be the bigger person and forgive her, and stop this nonsense as it's really upsetting her?'

As Ellen from our forum says: 'As for the whole "get over it" thing, I think that "get over it" has got to be one of my own Top Ten Most Hated Phrases Ever! I've heard it from my Enabling Father, who tells me to "get over" my "resentment" of my narcissistic mother who "did her best" (yeah, right – cobras are better mothers); from friends, who give me the whole "All parents make mistakes, you have to get over it ..."spiel; and even from my husband – although he at least is a little more understanding and tells me to "try to get over it for your own sake".'

How I *hate* that phrase! Hey, your own mother emotionally tormented / rejected / neglected / used / abused you, you grew up in a sick environment with no sense of what was normal or healthy, your whole life has been impacted by this; most people refuse to believe it even happened, and the person who did it to you feels no remorse and continues to claim that they did nothing wrong – so obviously the solution here is that *you* need to just "get over it"!'

The Flying Monkey will tell you how upset your mother is. 'You have hurt her so much. She doesn't know what she's done. She hasn't stopped crying since she got that letter. I am really worried about her. Her blood pressure has gone way up / asthma has got worse / stress is through the roof. Just come and talk to her, please. For her sake. For my sake. For your sake. For your children's sake – they need their grandmother.'

The Flying Monkey might also say, 'Well, you know, there are two sides to every story'. And this sounds plausible, and you, trying to be fair, might even start to agree with them. After all, you're only seeing your side, right?

Fact: when you're dealing with a narcissist, no, there are *not* two sides to the story. This is not a misunderstanding between two normal reasonable people. She is an abuser; you are an abuse victim, full stop.

Or they might say, 'How can you *do* this to your mother?' Indeed, you might be even saying this to yourself. And so their words have huge impact because they're speaking what you think yourself. But remember, you're not doing it *to* her. You're doing it for you, and any fallout she experiences is just Natural Consequences as we discussed before.

Another statement the Flying Monkey might make is, 'She misses you so much!' Indeed, your mother might say that herself if she writes to you.

She doesn't. She just does not. She misses her chew toy. That's all you are to her. Did you ever take a dead mouse from a cat? Did the cat miss the mouse? Sure. The cat probably meowed piteously and scratched around looking for the mouse. Does that mean the cat wanted a loving, mutually respecting relationship with the mouse?

Again, if you are truly NC you will not have heard this argument.

You will have politely but firmly told the Flying Monkey that you will not discuss this situation with them, that your decision is final and not up for debate.

And if you *have* heard this argument? Well, you have two options. You can then politely tell them that it doesn't make any difference. Or, you can agree to meet her to discuss it, and have her gaslight and invalidate etc, and you will realise you were right the first time, and then resume NC.

But do you take the point I'm trying to make? That there is no wrong way to do this. You can make a million mistakes, and still reclaim your NC. It's all okay. The only proviso is that if you give into a Flying Monkey's entreaties once, you'll have to work that bit harder to refuse them the next time, to convince them all that you really mean it this time. But that's okay too; you'll just do that.

Another option your narcissistic mother might take, especially if she's at the more malignant end of the spectrum, is to start a comprehensive Smearing Campaign. This is when she tells lies about you to everyone she can. And unfortunately she will sound convincing too. There might be enough of a grain of truth in it to make it sound credible.

And unfortunately many narcissists are very persuasive and so it's likely that most people will believe her. And there's nothing you can do – you won't know that she is saying this until people stop talking to you or are distant with you, and the damage is done then. (If they were the sort of people who would ask you for your side of the story before coming to a conclusion, then they'd already have done that.)

This tactic is especially tricky when used on the rest of your family. Narcissists rarely operate alone. They usually have a co-dependent enmeshed dynamic going on. And by daring to leave that dynamic, by daring to speak the truth, your narcissistic mother will make sure that they all turn on you. And they very possibly will.

And so, you have to accept the very real possibility that by going NC with your mother, you will lose the rest of your family too. Again, only you can decide if it is worth it to you – it's a tough decision, and one no one should have to make, but it's the kind of decision that is forced on us by the horrendous dynamic created by narcissists. We especially risk losing contact with our fathers.

A lot of DONMs struggle with going NC because it will mean losing contact with their father whom they still love. Yes, theoretically they could meet him independently of her, and it might be worth your while seeing if that is possible. But in pretty much all cases that I am aware of the father has been too much in the narcissistic mother's spell to agree to see his daughter independently. He will side with his wife regardless of his love for his daughter or her needs. And that makes sense because that is what he has done all his daughter's life after all; why should it change now?

And so, you will have to decide on whether you will put up with your mother for the sake of seeing your father, or not. It's an awful decision, and one that no one should be forced to make. But it is the reality.

One of the reasons DONMs give for not going NC is worry about what everyone will think of them. And in truth, there is no way, probably, to go NC and have everyone think you did the right thing.

The fact is that most people don't know about Narcissistic Personality Disorder. They either have not heard of it at all, or if they have, they dimly think it's something to do with extreme vanity. And so the narcissists are able to 'pass' among normal people, pretending to be like us, hiding among us. And only we few know about them.

To me it seems like a 1950s B-movie where the aliens have landed, are successfully pretending to be human, and only a few people realise the truth. And those few people are desperately telling the others, 'They're not real! They're aliens! Do you not get it?' and the others just dismiss the truth-tellers as being mad or crazy, and the aliens successfully continue their impersonation.

It truly is that difficult to tell the normal ones exactly what is going on with a narcissist. And so they, from their limited perspective, understandably think that you are being mean and nasty cutting off a perfectly lovely woman, and your mother to boot!

And so, you will most likely be vilified and lambasted for that decision, and there's not much you can do about it. Again, only you can decide if the price of being in touch with her is worth keeping the relatively good opinion of these people.

If you delete and ignore enough, eventually she will most likely get the hint. The trick is not to respond at all, even to reiterate your demands to be left alone. If you do that, you're just teaching her that you *can* be made to react, and so she'll continue her campaign.

Occasionally narcissistic mothers do not give up, and their hoovering becomes sheer stalking. In this case you need to get police advice and see what legal recourse you have towards solving this – a restraining order or similar.

Effects of No Contact

When DONMs go NC they can experience a range of benefits immediately. Many report just feeling happier, lighter, less stressed. They find that they are taking better care of themselves – getting haircuts, manicures, etc. Many lose excess weight without even trying now that they're no longer comfort eating to help them cope with their mother. Others find that they are more creative – ideas come to them, their crafts or art just flows better. They feel better about themselves, which again makes sense as they are no longer being consistently run down.

However, sometimes it is not so easy. Yes, those gifts await. But sometimes there are challenges before you receive them.

There is the bereavement mentioned previously. That is very real.

Also, after going NC huge guilt can kick in too. It's easy to forget how bad your mother is and start minimising what she has done to you. This is not surprising as minimising is what we were taught to do all our lives. And, again society doesn't help with its insistence on worshipping the cult of The Mother.

To get over guilt I have a few suggestions. The first is to use the EFT script on page 179 for erasing that guilt.

The second is to read the section on Beliefs on page 120. Your guilt is based on false beliefs. The guilt is *real* but it is not *justified*. And then, as you experience guilt, observe that feeling. Allow it to be. Do not fight it, do not resist it, do not think it's wrong. It is what it is. All feelings are fine. (I know, again, that your mother taught you differently, but she was wrong about that as about so much else.)

So, observe the feeling of guilt, but yet do not swim in it or become submerged in it. The act of observing it will distance you from it. Tune into yourself and see where in your body you are holding it – e.g. a tension in your chest, a stone in your stomach, and just observe that.

You can even talk to the guilt as per the dialogue suggested below. I know this might seem strange, but in reality you are just talking to the part of yourself which is experiencing the guilt. You will see that the dialogue I suggest is courteous and even grateful. This is because this guilt is not the enemy. It is you trying to help you based on the information it has.

You can say, 'Hello, Guilt. I see you. I acknowledge you. Thank you for coming to try to help me. I know you want me to do the right thing. And you think the right thing is to send her a birthday card. But you know, that is not so. That is wrong information. The right thing for me is to mind myself and protect myself from an abuser.'

The third suggestion is to write your story as advised on page 133. (Or, if you have written it, to re-read it.) This will remind you of why you are NC and stop you minimising her actions. One member of our forum, Janet, even wrote the Top Ten list of her mother's horrendous actions, and attached them with a magnet to her fridge (folded over so that she did not read them by mistake). That way they were there and handy for her to read if she was ever tempted to phone her mother.

Quite apart from bereavement and guilt, NC can simply feel strange. You might feel very out-of-sorts and not know why. Confused. Discombobulated. This is because you have been under the weight of the dysfunction for so long that it can feel strange without it. And because you were referencing your mother (and her likes, and dislikes, and possible annoyances, and need for attention) with regard to so much in your life – now you are not doing that, and it feels odd. You are like someone coming off a ship and finding it strange to walk on solid ground until they get used to it.

You might also miss the drama. Even though you are not a drama addict like your mother, it's what you're used to. Life can seem very quiet and boring without it. I suggest you ask yourself honestly if this is so. If it is, just remind yourself that drama is by its nature disturbing and destructive, that life brings enough of its own dramas without creating more, and know that you will get used to this too, and enjoy the peace in time.

For now, just accept the strange feeling, in much the same way as you accept how it feels strange to wear new shoes until it doesn't feel strange any more. You will get used to this new way of being, gradually and imperceptibly.

What do you say to people about the fact you're No Contact?

This is a tricky one. Because of society's belief that we should all stay in touch with our mother, no matter how abusive she is – or even more so, because society still cannot accept that mothers can be abusive – it's not easy to explain. And you don't want to get into explaining anyway, most likely. It's no one's business really. I tend to try to tell people the truth, if it's appropriate. This is because it is my passion to inform the world about NPD (hence my website, forum and this book), and that would not apply to you, most likely.

The trick is to remember that you have no need to *JADE*. That is, no need to Justify, Argue, Defend or Explain your reasons. You don't have to convince the other person that you were right to do what you did.

So, depending on the situation, you can give more or less information. You can just say lightly (to colleagues say, who want to know if you're going to see your parents for Christmas), 'No. My parents and I are estranged.' And then change the subject.

To others, say your mother-in-law, or your best friend, you can explain a bit more. You can say, 'My mother has an incurable personality disorder that makes her consistently mistreat and abuse me. This disorder also means that she is not open to change or to treating me better, so my only option is to remove myself. I realise you will find that hard to understand, but I do ask you to trust me in this, to believe that I did not come to this decision lightly, and, if you cannot support this decision, at least do not undermine it.'

If they are interested enough, they can read this book.

What do you tell your children about No Contact?

A big challenge with going No Contact is what to tell your children. This will depend on their age and on the relationship they had with your mother, so this advice can only be general.

Many DONMs start off by thinking that they have to allow their children to stay in touch with their parents. After all, goes the thinking, it would be totally wrong to deprive children of their grandparents.

If you have this mindset, I do offer you the suggestion that you could re-evaluate this. Yes, in an ideal situation your children will have grandparents. But you do not find yourself in an ideal situation or anything like it. Your mother is an *abuser*. She is toxic, i.e. poisonous. And the poison, while metaphorical rather than literal, is very, very real. Look at the effect she has had on you.

You have every right, and indeed, the responsibility, to protect your children from abusers no matter who they are. Even though society possibly gives grandparents a higher iconic status even than mothers; even so, if the grandparents are abusers, your children need to be protected from them.

You are teaching your children that when no compromise can be worked out with a difficult person, you must go on your way, for your own health and sanity. Also you are teaching them that just because someone is a family member, it is not ok for them to abuse you and get away with it. These are valuable lessons for children to learn.

If your mother is an Ignoring Grandmother, as mine was, then there is little or no difficulty. My son, who was 12 at the time, literally sagged with relief when he heard he'd never have to see her or my father again.

But the challenge is when your Narcissistic Mother is engulfing, as they often are with young grandchildren. Sometimes the narcissistic mothers can make really good grandparents to young children, who in turn adore them. You might hesitate to break this bond, understandably so. There are a couple of things to consider though about this:

- It is very possible that once your child reaches the age where she starts saying no to her Gran, or expressing opinions, or in any way becoming her own person (you know, the sort of thing normal people *celebrate!*), often around the age of 7, that your mother will turn on her and become narcissistically nasty to her. So better to cut off the contact now, if that's the case, rather than set your child up for a bigger fall later.
- The Engulfing Narcissistic Grandmothers can actually come between you and your children, and this is very serious. There have been cases on our forum where the narcissistic mother literally took over the child, either as a child, or when they were

adult, because of the grooming they were able to do during their childhood. They do this by spoiling the child with sweets and toys etc, undermining the parenting by saying things like, 'Don't mind what Mummy said, I'll let you do it'. In this way an innocent child might come to prefer Grandma to you, seeing as Grandma is fun and treats and sweets, and you are green vegetables and bedtimes. Some narcissistic mothers even get the grandchild to call *her* Mummy, and you by your first name.

- It's very possible that the relationship is subtly abusive anyway. Maybe your narcissistic mother is playing favourites, with a Golden Child and a Scapegoat dynamic going on among your children. Or playing the usual narcissistic tricks on your child, even as she's spoiling and wooing them.
- The most important thing your child needs is for you to be happy and whole. Despite what your narcissistic mother told you, your needs *do* matter. Not instead of your child's needs, of course. However, your child does not *need* the relationship with her grandmother, but she does need a happy and whole *you*. So if No Contact is what you need for your well-being and sanity, then that's the right thing for the whole family.

So, how do you explain No Contact to a small child? You can just distract them, and if they ask about going to see Nana, just say that you're not going that day, and over time they will most likely stop asking.

My own opinion though is that this is not ideal. I don't think it's a good idea for people to just disappear without explanation from a child's life, because that can be very scary for them. Who's next, they might wonder?

And so I would suggest explaining gently, 'We are not going to see Grandma for a while. She is very mean and nasty to Mummy, and won't say sorry or stop being mean. And we don't let mean people play with us, so until she is nice, we won't be seeing her.'

To me this gives the child a good explanation, and also teaches her about boundaries and about not letting people abuse you. Be sure to emphasise though that you have to be *very* mean, over a period of time, and never ever say sorry, lest the child worries that she would be cast out for some tiny misdemeanour.

With older children you can go into more detail, telling them about NPD. It's most likely that older children will have spotted some of her oddnesses already. Be careful not to parentify your child, i.e. putting the burden of your own pain on them. But information is good. And there are narcissists in the world so your children will encounter them, so this information is valuable to them anyway.

What about siblings?

Many DONMs resist going NC because they feel responsible for siblings. This can be one of the most heart-breaking aspects of the situation. We can feel like we're abandoning them. And indeed, in many cases, this might be so, especially if there are younger siblings still living at home. It is one of many no-win situations created by these narcissistic mothers. The thing is, there's nothing else we can do. We can't help a drowning person by drowning ourselves. The best we can hope for is that our freedom and our happiness makes them realise it's possible, and to aspire to that themselves.

I do have to say, though, that it is much more likely that your narcissistic mother will smear you so convincingly to your siblings that they will reject you.

Dysfunctional families hate the truth-tellers, the whistle-blowers. They are all about admiring the Emperor's new clothes, and they turn on anyone who dares to mention the nakedness.

And the Golden Child will not wish to risk her position, and if you were the Golden Child, a former Scapegoat might well be elevated to the position of Golden Child in your place, and that is very difficult to resist.

So yes, in going NC you risk losing your whole family. This is awful – but is the cold clear reality of the situation.

'But what if she dies? Won't you feel guilty about NC then?'

This is a question that comes up whenever you consider NC. You will either consider it yourself, but also you may be sure others will say it to you when they hear your situation.

Here's the thing: she *will* die. It's not *if*, it's *when*.

And will you feel guilty then that you didn't see her for the last however-many years of her life? Will you feel like a bad daughter, a bad person, for rejecting her all those years, and then she died and now it's too late? Could you live with yourself? Could you bear the guilt?

Only you can answer this of course. And it's true that if you remain in contact you will not have to deal with this issue. And that would be a very valid reason for you to remain in contact, if that's what you choose. There would be a high price for that, of course, but you may well consider it worth paying.

Another perspective to consider, however, is that the fact that she will die as all living things do, isn't a Get Out of Jail Free card to allow her to continue abusing you. It doesn't mean that you need to continue putting up with abuse. You deserve better.

And any guilt you would feel after she had died would be false guilt. As we have touched on before, guilt is for when you do something wrong. Protecting yourself from an abuser is not wrong.

What about a death-bed call? She is dying, and is asking for you. What then?

I have not experienced this myself, as of yet, so I cannot say for sure what I would do. But I know what I believe I will do, and what I am determined to do. And that is to ignore the call. She has had years and years to genuinely sort out this situation with me, and has ignored those opportunities. (And truly, in such a case, where does any guilt rightfully rest? Not with me.)

A death-bed meeting cannot end well. She, being narcissistic, will most likely not take the opportunity to own what she did and genuinely apologise. If she did, I would of course accept the apology and we could part as friends. But it is not going to happen. She has had years to do it, and has not done so. (She will tell you she has tried to sort things out. She has, over the years, sent birthday cards and Christmas texts. She is, no doubt, saying, and even believing, that she is keeping the door open and I am the one being stubborn and obdurate. But she has never once said, 'What was wrong, and how can we fix it?')

So, I can imagine the death-bed scene involving her saying she is sorry we were estranged (fauxpology) and that she wanted us to make up before it was too late. The only way it would be drama-free, as I see it, would be for me to accept that lie and play along. And I will not do that. I would definitely regret that for the rest of my life; it would be a bitter stone in my stomach that I would carry forever. To assist her in invalidating the experience of my whole life would hurt me irrevocably and I would not do it. Now that I know the truth, I will not tell a lie about it.

And so my only other option would be to speak my truth. And she would begin gaslighting and lying and invalidating of course, and most definitely including tearful references to the fact she's dying. It would be extremely fraught and painful and upsetting, and I do not need that. And even more so, a dying woman does not need that.

And so, I see it as a kindness and a courtesy that I do not go to her deathbed. Because the 'I' that would go would not be the 'I' she knew, which was the one who colluded in her lies to keep the peace. The 'I' that would be there would be the woman I am now, who would speak her truth. And my mother does not want that 'I' at her deathbed, even though she doesn't realise it.

Others will vilify me for it, no doubt. The death-bed reconciliation is such a staple in our culture, to reject it is so taboo, that I will be judged harshly for it. So be it. That is the price I pay for avoiding the two impossible options of having to either collude in my own gaslighting, or distress a dying woman.

I also believe that I will not go to her or my father's funeral. It would seem hypocritical to go. And if I do go it would put me in one of two impossible situations. I either collude in more lies by accepting mourners' commiserations and condolences. Or I tell them bluntly the truth and thereby distress them. They don't need that, nor deserve it. So it is a kindness to them, quite apart from the right thing for me, that I do not go.

These facts bring me no joy. I think it is heart-breaking that I am in a position of not attending my mother's death-bed or funeral. But that is the situation that she has created. It is none of my doing.

Another side-effect of No Contact

One very frequent side-effect of NC is that after a little while you start to look at your other relationships. This will not be a conscious decision; it'll happen by itself. And this might not be easy at all because you might well realise that you have other narcissists in your life. Your husband or partner maybe. Friends.

This is very very tough. You can feel very alone and upset. Is *everyone* a narcissist?

No. Only 0.6 per cent – 1 per cent.

But it's very possible that you have surrounded yourself with a fair proportion of that 1 per cent. It makes sense. It's what you knew, after all. It's what felt comfortable in a strange way. And the narcissists probably found it much easier to hook you than they would someone else who had been raised normally.

What you do is, of course, up to you, as ever. But you might find that you want to cut the ties with these other narcissists too. After all, you're in a different place now. You know that you deserve to be treated well. You know that you deserve to be in healthy relationships.

But still … but still ….

You are reeling from the enormity of cutting off your mother, and possibly your whole family. The thought of losing more people out of your life is just terrifying. You will have no one then.

And of course the thought occurs, is it *you?* If you are having difficulty getting on with your whole circle, well it must be you, right. Maybe some people in your circle are even saying that to you. And of course, as a DONM you're used to being blamed, and even blaming yourself, when things go wrong, so it's easy to believe.

But no, it's not you. It's just that you surrounded yourself with narcissists, and no one assertive can get on with them.

So you might well find that there is a major house-clearing to be done to get rid of those toxic relationships too. Many DONMs find this.

It's hugely challenging and terrifying, there is no denying that.

But here are a few things to remember: you don't have to do it immediately. Take your time. It can wait till you're stronger. And you won't be left isolated, because getting rid of the toxic ones will leave room for healthy people to come in. And in a kind of alchemy, when you make that absolute decision that you will not put up with being maltreated, other people seem to sense that somehow, and it repels the toxic ones and attracts the healthier ones.

It takes courage to cut off most or all of the people in your life. Huge courage. But the gifts are enormous. You will no longer have people demeaning you and bringing you down and abusing you. You will have room for healthy people who support you and empower you.

You might be wondering, too, how to avoid narcissists in future, and not let them even invade your life in the first place. The good news is that once you know about narcissism you do tend to get a sense of them. I can spot a narcissist at a hundred paces now! But here are some ways to test if someone is a narcissist:

- Ask them for a favour and see how they react. Obviously make it a reasonable favour, a favour appropriate to whatever relationship you have with them. A normal person will do it without thought.

A narcissist will either wriggle out of it, or do it begrudgingly, or do it overly-keenly and then make sure to ask you for another favour soon, in order to redress the balance.

- Equally, refuse a request they make of you. Do it kindly and politely of course. A normal person will respect your right to say no. A narcissist will not, and will react badly.

- Or, calmly, but emphatically, disagree with an opinion they express. And see how they react. A normal person is quite happy to agree to disagree, unless it's a very emotive topic for them, so maybe choose a more banal topic. Something like the best song or film, rather than say, abortion or religion. A narcissist will not be a bit happy with you disagreeing and will get miffed, or try to argue with you, or otherwise not let it go.

- Or, try, as an experiment, to keep the conversation on you rather than them. A narcissist will never allow that.

6
ARE YOU NARCISSISTIC?

You probably won't be long on this journey before the horrific thought hits you – what if *you* are narcissistic?

You think of all the times you've treated your children less than well, or times you talked too much, the way your mother does. And of course, here you are obsessing about yourself, as you read this book, by thinking about yourself and your childhood and adult experiences. What is all that if not narcissistic?

I have good news for you:

If you are genuinely fretting and worrying that you might be narcissistic, you're not. It's a bit of a paradox in a way, but it does make sense.

Think of it this way – a narcissist *never* thinks badly of herself, or questions herself. She would never even consider that she could be less than perfect. So she would never think that she could be narcissistic, and by corollary, if you worry that you are, you're not.

It's okay to think of yourself and be concerned with your own doings and concerns. That is *not* narcissistic. It's not surprising we think so, though. In a complete irony, our narcissistic mothers teach us, by word and deed, that it's wrong of *us* to be concerned about our own concerns. Of course she did. The only ones whose concerns matter is – drum roll please – *hers*!

Of course that's not true. The truth is that our concerns *are* valid, and it's *not* narcissistic to be involved with those.

We touched on this before, but it's appropriate to repeat: *Sometimes it really is about me.* And in that case it's appropriate for the attention to be on me. My wedding. My marriage break-up. My illness. My miscarriage. My publishing deal. My birthday party.

And equally, sometimes it really is about the other person, and in that case it is *not* about me, except to the extent that I can be a support and cheerleader for the person who it is about. Their wedding. Their marriage break-up. Their illness. Their miscarriage.

And you know, normal people find it easy to divide the *appropriate–that–it's–about–me* occasions from the *appropriate–that–it's–about–them* occasions.

For narcissists it's a non-issue. For them, as you know, *all* occasions *are* about them, no exceptions.

For us DONMs, we can tend to go to the other extreme, partly because that's what our narcissistic mother taught us, and partly out of a fear of being like her.

So I am telling you now that it's fine, and not in the slightest narcissistic, to claim the occasions that are appropriately about you. At the beginning you might have to consciously ask yourself which occasions fall into that category, rather than automatically knowing. But it'll come with practice. And it might feel strange at the start – but just accept the strange feeling and go with it anyway, I suggest. As you do it, it'll feel less strange until you're doing it like a pro.

Fleas

One issue you might have, however, is narcissistic tendencies or behaviours without being narcissistic at all. We call these *fleas*, because you catch them, i.e. learn them, from your narcissistic mother. We all learn so much from our parents about how to behave with others. And if what is modelled for us is narcissistic behaviour, then that's all we know what to do.

So, for example, we might be over-sensitive when it comes to constructive criticism. This is because we never got constructive criticism from our narcissistic mother. We got shaming, soul-destroying, criticism designed to put is back in our box.

And so, maybe now whenever you get constructive well-meant criticism, you do over-react. It feels like an attack, even though it's not. But you never knew any differently.

There is an irony, isn't there, in our mothers gaslighting us by telling us we're over-sensitive, and then creating a situation in which we *are* over-sensitive.

Another example of fleas might be chronic lying. It's very possible that it wasn't safe to tell the truth to your narcissistic mother. And so lying became a way of staying safe. And in later years you're still doing it, automatically, because telling the truth feels dangerous. (See the section on beliefs on page 120 for more on this)

Let me give you another example of fleas from my own life.

Whenever my mother would get annoyed, she would go into this elaborate pantomime of upset. There'd be lots of sulks and sniffs and snapped comments.

And so you'd ask how she was and she'd snap, 'Fine!' in that tone of voice which clearly meant, 'Anything but fine'.

So you'd say, 'What's wrong?' (because you knew better than to accept her answer on face value), and get a snapped, 'Nothing!' in that tone which clearly meant, 'Lots!'

So then you'd have to run around her (lots of narcissistic supply there, of course) absolutely *cajoling* her and begging her to tell you what was wrong. Which of course, turned out to be something *you* had done wrong. So it was like asking a condemned prisoner to weave his own rope.

Ugh.

But here's the thing – when I got married, guess what I used to do if I was upset with my husband about any behaviour?

Yep, exactly that.

I wasn't doing it in a manipulative way ... it was just that that was all I knew. I had never learned any other way of relating or raising issues. It never even occurred to me that it was possible to say calmly, 'Hey, when you did X it upset me for Y reason, can we discuss that?'

Except, not being narcissistic, after a few years it occurred to me that this was not the way to do things. So I changed how I dealt with things that upset me.

That's the difference between a flea and full-blown narcissistic behaviour. With a flea you can a) recognise that it's inappropriate, and b) choose therefore to change the behaviour, and c) actually change it. Changing it might be difficult as it's an ingrained habit, but if it's a flea you keep going until you manage.

A narcissist wouldn't even get as far as step A, after all!

It's very possible that you have fleas too. I think it's impossible to live with a narcissist and not pick some up. So the next step, if you think you might, is to examine your own reactions and responses, and see if they are appropriate and high-functioning behaviours. And perhaps ask those close to you to comment (in a loving and gentle way) on things you do that they find challenging.

And once you've identified these behaviours, simply change them. And seeing as you are not a narcissist, you'll be able to do that. Some of them won't be easy to change, as they're ingrained. But they're all possible to change, especially with the help of EFT.

7
YOUR PROGRAMMED BELIEFS

We spoke earlier about the various ways in which being raised by a narcissist impacts on us. The reason it continues to impact us even into adulthood is because our beliefs have been programmed, and we act automatically based on our beliefs. And just like a computer program, until they are changed our beliefs will stay the same and so the behaviour will stay the same. And of course, then, the outcome will stay the same.

But the good news is that, again like a computer program, your beliefs can be changed.

Here's how it works:

When babies are born, the neurons in their brains are unconnected. A huge amount of the work they do in infancy is to forge connections between these neurons.

They do this by gathering evidence about how the world works, and coming to conclusions about it, and establishing the connections based on that.

This system works very well. For example, the child gets to establish a connection between the experience of an actual dog, and the word 'dog' – and that's how they learn language.

You can sometimes see this system in action when a child comes to the wrong conclusion, and a lot of fun we get out of young children is based on these mistakes. For instance, when my son was about six he told me very seriously that French people spell differently than we do, because they spell the word 'the' as 'ze'. And he once drew a picture of a pirate ship, and pointed out to me, 'There's the Captain, and there,' he said, pointing to the crew, 'are the hearties', – because he heard stereotypical pirate captains say, 'Ahoy, me hearties!' and came to the logical, but incorrect, conclusion that the crew were called hearties!

If a child is loved well, and her needs are met, she gathers that evidence and comes to the logical conclusion that she is a valuable, lovable, worthwhile person.

If, however, she is not loved enough, if she's neglected and shamed, she's going to draw a conclusion about that too. And she is, for good reason, going to draw the conclusion that she's not loved enough because she's not loveable. She is neglected because she's not worth looking after. She is shamed because she's shameful.

The reason she comes to this conclusion rather than, say, to pick a wild example, the conclusion that her mother is damaged or flawed, is simple. Children absolutely need their parents to be good. This is a deep psychological need, and it makes sense. Parents are children's means of survival, and so they need to think of them as competent and good and strong. So all evidence to the contrary must be interpreted in some way that does not compromise that belief.

And so, all that is left is to blame herself, the child, for why she isn't loved, or cared for etc.

And that is the belief that gets programmed into her brain.

It makes sense, doesn't it?

And of course, that is exactly what happened to us, as daughters of narcissistic mothers. We came to beliefs about the world, and about ourselves, based on the evidence. We came to reasonable, logical, sensible conclusions about that. But, they were conclusions that were ultimately wrong.

The real reason you weren't loved is not because you weren't loveable, but because your mother is a narcissist and so is incapable of love.

Now, you may believe this rationally, just not in your gut. You may know it in your head but not feel it. Or, you may not even know it in your head. It's okay either way. Because the good news is that these beliefs can be changed. They really can. You can come to know, with every fibre of your being, that you are loveable, and not being loved was your mother's lack, not yours.

And so – and this is *very* important – the fact that beliefs can be wrong means that your brain often lies to you. We are used to trusting our thoughts, but truly we cannot always. The brain can be fooled. This is the very reason that our narcissistic mothers manage to confuse us at all – if our brains always accurately knew reality, then she would never be able to convince us that her version was the right version.

So, our beliefs, and hence our thoughts, are often inaccurate. This might seem scary, and it is a bit, in truth. Where, then, is our security? The trick is to check our thoughts against the truth. And to remember something which at first thought seems really bad but which is good news really, and is very empowering:

Just because you think a thought, doesn't automatically mean it's true.

Now, it feels true. Of course it does. But it is not necessarily true. And since our feelings are guided by our beliefs, there's a belief underlying each feeling.

So if you feel guilty at not being in touch with your mother, the belief behind that is: *A daughter should be in touch with her mother, and I am wrong for not doing so.* And that belief is not true. A daughter does not have to be in touch with a toxic, abusive mother.

And if you feel you should send her a birthday card, the belief behind that is: *A daughter should send her mother a birthday card.* But is that belief true?

These beliefs lead into negative self-talk. One of the many legacies that our narcissistic mothers give us is that of negative self-talk. It's as if her voice – her shrill, insulting, demeaning voice – got lodged in our head, and remains there. And that voice provides a running commentary to everything we do, and it's not exactly a nice supportive commentary, is it?

'Oh you really think you can do that? Ha!'

'You'll never amount to anything.'

'See, you made another mistake! I don't know why you even bother.'

'You're useless.'

'You're ugly. No one will ever desire you.'

And on and on and on. There are a million lyrics to this particular song, aren't there? And they're all painful.

In a further irony, you may not even be aware of this negative self-talk. Not really. It's so much a part of you, and comes so quickly and sneakily, that you are probably not conscious of it.

You just find that you are behaving in ways that respond to that voice. You don't apply for that job, you don't respond when someone tries to flirt with you, you don't bother going to that party. In a thousand ways you listen to that voice and act on its message.

Thing is, that voice tells lies. Our narcissistic mother told us a million small lies along with The Big Lie. Smaller, maybe, but no less damaging for you.

These are the lies she tells you about who you are. The details of the lies will vary, but they are all designed to keep you trapped, and weak, and under her control.

So statements like, 'You'll never amount to anything', or 'You have no judgement, you always make stupid decisions' come into this category.

I'm sure you can make your own list of similar statements that you were told.

In addition, narcissists are masters of projection as we mentioned above in the section on narcissistic mothers' traits. So the lies which come into this category would include things which are actually true for her rather than us, like:

'You're over-sensitive.'

'Nothing pleases you.'

'You're so hard to get along with.'

There is a lifetime of all these little lies about who you are, which means that you end up with all these beliefs which make up your own mental map about who you are.

Thing is:

THEY'RE NOT TRUE!

Or if one or two of them are a bit true, such as in fleas, it's not because your narcissistic mother perceptively spotted it. She doesn't see you well enough to see your real faults. It's because it's coincidentally true. Even a stopped clock is right, by accident, twice a day, after all.

So, the take-away from this issue is this:

Don't believe one word out of your mother's mouth. Probably not about anything, but especially about who you are.

SHE DOESN'T KNOW WHO YOU ARE!

She doesn't observe you as you. She doesn't care. You're not a real person to her. (Nothing personal; no one is.)

And so, her opinion of who you are is – *has to be!* – totally flawed.

So you don't have to believe a word of it.

Sure, own your flaws, and your fleas, and seek to improve upon them. But get feedback about them from people other than your mother – partners and friends, once they're trustworthy and genuinely have your best interests at heart.

Don't believe one word about yourself out of your mother's mouth. This is essential.

To erase this belief, use the Tapping Affirmation on page 154.

The false image and beliefs she gave you both manifest as a little voice – the negative self-talk we mentioned already.

The first thing is to become *aware* of the voice. Try to listen to yourself consciously, and hear what messages you are getting. This is probably the hardest step, and you'll fail again and again – the voice will slip out of your conscious awareness.

But that's okay. Remember that it's okay not to be perfect. Everyone is bad at a new skill when they start learning it. Have you ever seen a baby learn to walk? She falls again and again and again and again. But she doesn't get upset, she just gets up again and tries again. And over time she manages a step more before she falls, and in such steps (literally!) she becomes a proficient walker. The same applies to every skill, and this is a new skill.

The second, and hugely important thing, is to know that this voice is actually part of *you*. Yes, it speaks your mother's words, and probably even in her tone or her voice, but it's part of *you*.

And even more bizarrely, it's a part of you that is trying to help you. All parts of you, even the sabotaging ones, are always doing their best to help. It's trying to help you, but it's doing it wrongly, because that's all it knows. That's the message it received. How can it know any better?

But because it's part of you, and your friend, and is trying to help you, then don't get upset with it. Don't get frustrated. Be gentle.

This voice just has wrong information, that's all. Wrong information about who you are. It's not your enemy, it's your friend with wrong information.

And so, when you hear this wrong message with this wrong voice, I suggest you observe the voice. Observe the message. Be aware of it, and consciously notice it.

Say to yourself, 'Oh, I'm now thinking that I'll never amount to anything. That's the thought that is now going on.'

By observing it objectively like that, you remove yourself from it a bit. You're not swimming in that thought, believing it, living it. You're stepping to one side and noticing it.

And in noticing it, you can judge it, assess it, discern its objective truth.

And what you do then is to say to the voice, kindly but firmly (like to a recalcitrant puppy): 'Voice, I know you're trying to help me, and I appreciate that. But you're actually wrong about what you're saying. That is wrong information. It is not true that I'll never amount to anything. The true belief is that I might amount to something. That we don't know yet. That it's worth trying. That there is value and growth and learning in the trying regardless of the outcome. I know you want to help me, and the way to help me is to give me your help and support in this.'

Do you see how you speak to it, to change its 'truths' – which are really only its beliefs? And how you give it a new, better, truer truth. Not an unreasonable one. Don't get it to believe that you will definitely amount to lots – because that's a step too far. So create a truth that is really true and which supports the effort, such as my example above.

This process does work, but can be slow. The Voice will be slow to change its 'truths'. They are very entrenched after all.

The quick way to deal with these beliefs is to use EFT on them, as per the instructions on page 143. It will literally erase them quicker than you can imagine now, and replace them with true, empowering beliefs.

The joy of being wrong

One important element of what I'm sharing here is the revolutionary thought that:

It's good to be wrong!

What would you like to be wrong about?

- I'm wrong about the fact that I'm unlovable.
- I'm wrong about being over-sensitive.
- I'm wrong about being crazy.
- I'm wrong about owing her anything.
- I'm wrong about not being good enough.

- I'm wrong about the power she has over me.

And so on and so on. In fact, as a DONM, you (and I) are wrong about so many things. This is not surprising, as all our lives we were taught pure lies. (Added to the normal human tendency to misjudge things and be wrong about stuff.)

And every single time you learn you're wrong, you have the opportunity for growth. It means that you are more than you ever were before. Stronger, wiser, all sorts of good things. Which, of course, will never happen for your narcissistic mother – as she's never wrong, she can never, and will never, grow as a person.

And in truth, in order to achieve anything in life we need to allow ourselves to make mistakes, to be wrong as it were. Creation is messy; it's a process of elimination and trial and error. And that's okay! The more we can be comfortable with that, the more powerful we are.

But ...

Being wrong can feel so threatening, can't it?

I think it's because the narcissistic mother's Big Lie that we had to be perfect for her to love us.

Of course, being uncomfortable being wrong is another thing you're wrong about! And once you can be comfortable being wrong, you can let that feeling go too. Except that it's not that easy, is it? It's like pulling yourself up by your bootstraps!

Well again, EFT is the solution, and it's on page 182. I have done a lot of work on this issue with EFT, and I cannot tell you the difference it makes. I now have very little ego attachment to being right. I prefer to be right, of course! I try and make it my business to make right decisions and come to right conclusions and have right information and so on – because doing all those things makes life much better and easier. This does not make me careless in any way.

But I'm always open to the possibility that I'm wrong about stuff, and it doesn't hurt me when I learn that I am. I don't feel *less–than* because I was wrong. I am able to take off the wrong opinion / belief with as little trauma as removing an old worn-out pair of shoes, and putting on the new shiny shoes that I can admire and enjoy. Being wrong is something I *do,* not something I *am.* And therefore it does not reflect badly on me to be wrong (just as it doesn't reflect well on me to be right), so it's easy for me to own when I am wrong.

And I so would like you to have that same experience, because, in all honesty, it makes everything else possible. All our hang-ups and sabotaging behaviour and fears and limitations are down to our beliefs, and the more easily we can let go of wrong beliefs, the easier we can access new, better behaviours – and more easily we can improve our quality of life.

And that's what it's about, isn't it?

Improving our quality of life.

Part Two
HOW TO HEAL

ABOUT HEALING

Now that you realise the truth about what was done to you, it's time to consider your healing. What happened to you, i.e., the damage that was done to you by your narcissistic mother (or parents) is not your fault. What is your responsibility is the healing part (if you choose you want that, of course), fixing the damage that you didn't cause. It's so unfair that we have to do it, that it takes us so much time and energy to get to a place most people begin from. But it's the reality of the toxic legacy.

The information I have given you so far will hopefully help you to understand your past, and the legacy that being raised by a narcissist has given you. But I truly believe that this knowledge does not have to be just theoretical, that we can heal. We are lucky that we live at a time when there are techniques which can help us heal more quickly than previous generations could have hoped for.

What I have come to learn is that there are two distinct elements that are essential for DONMs. The first is to speak your truth. That is something we were totally denied in the toxic relationship with our mothers. We had access only to her version of truth-lite, so to speak. I think it's essential to speak your truth, to say in essence, 'Yes, this did happen. This is what really happened no matter how she lied, gaslighted and spun it to be different.' There is more about speaking your truth below.

The second essential element is, once you have spoken your truth, to move on. Now, how long you stay in the first stage is up to you. You may need to speak your truth a number of times. The trouble is, the danger is, that you fall into a victim status and stay there. And that does not empower you or improve your life at all.

So what I hope to share here is both the advisability of moving on and healing, and the tools to allow you to do so.

You truly do deserve the best life possible, the life she tried to rob you of.

And it's so true what they say, the best revenge is living well.

So that said, here are my thoughts on how to live well.

8
CLAIM YOUR TRUTH

I recommend that you write out your story.

It is better to hand-write it rather than type or dictate it. There is something very powerful and kinaesthetic about the physical act of hand-writing. It gets you in touch with your subconscious very well. If you physically cannot hand-write then typing is of course a possibility, but it is a poor second-best. At this stage I do not suggest just speaking your truth as it is not physical or kinaesthetic enough.

So, get yourself a notebook. You're best getting the cheapest and most ordinary one you can. Not a fancy one with a fancy cover that would demand that you live up to it with perfect prose and poetic words. This is about getting down and dirty, and telling it like it is, and you need to feel comfortable doing that.

But what if you don't know what to write? What if you sit in front of this notebook and no words come? Well then, I recommend a process called freewriting. What you do is set a timer for 15 minutes, and you sit down at the notebook and you start writing words, and – this is essential – you do not stop for the 15 minutes! But, equally essential, *it does not matter what you write.* You get out of judgement about that, and just write away. If you end up spending 15 minutes writing over and over, 'I don't know what to write, I don't know what to write', then that's okay.

That most likely won't apply, though. What'll happen is that you start hooking into your subconscious and words will come to you.

So you might end up writing something like the following (and note the lack of punctuation in this, as it just flowed), 'I don't know what to write I don't know what to write I'm supposed to be writing about my mother but I don't know what to say about her I suppose I could say what a bitch she is and how much I hate her, but I can't say that but why not, it's true, look at all she did to me as a child, there was that time she did x ...'.

Do you see how the discussion between various parts of your brain started coming in? In this example I started to acknowledge she was a bitch and I hated her, but then I censored myself, but then I started giving myself permission to write that.

Now I stress that this is only an example! There is no right or wrong way to do this. I know that as DONMs we are prone to be very critical of ourselves and to try to live up to some impossible standard. So to have an exercise where there is no wrong way to do it, is possibly scary and intimidating. But truly, the only way to do it wrong is to stop writing. Once you keep that pen moving and write whatever comes, you are doing it right. This is a dialogue between you and you – how can it be wrong?

Very rarely you might find that you have to spend a number of 15 minute sessions writing 'I don't know what to write' over and over, before the words start coming. That can happen if, in your brain, the injunction to never speak your truth is very solid. But do persevere – this exercise holds so much freedom and power within it.

Now, this process can be tough. There can be pain; these memories will not necessarily be pleasant. Well, probably they will *not* be pleasant. If you get upset while you are writing, if at all possible keep writing through the pain. Just accept the pain and allow it. If it really does get too much, stop writing and tap, i.e. use EFT. This is very powerful healing, because these feelings, which had been buried and submerged all these years, are now being experienced and acknowledged and felt, and with the help of EFT, processed and moved on.

9
WHAT ABOUT FORGIVING HER?

I discuss forgiving her here, as it is, if anything, an element in your own healing. But forgiveness is a loaded topic.

During my last conversation with my mother she said, sulkily almost, crossly for sure, 'You won't forgive us'. The subtext being, as I had heard this many times before, 'You are so begrudging and hard that you cling to your upset'. Which of course was invalidation all by itself. And the subtext of *that* was, 'You need to keep writing off all that we do, and allow us to keep doing it'.

I pointed this out to her by saying, 'If by "forgive", you mean to allow you to keep abusing me, then you're right, I won't forgive you. But I am not bearing any grudges.' Needless to say, in classic narcissist form she didn't engage with that and just repeated, 'You won't forgive us!'

Was she right? Should I have forgiven her and my father? What does forgiveness even mean?

This issue comes up regularly for DONMs, and is a fraught one. There are two challenges with it. The first is a question as to whether narcissists can help what they do, and if not, should they be blamed for doing what they can't help. We don't blame people with Tourette's, for example, for doing things which would we would blame other people for doing. People with Tourette's don't need forgiveness for their expletives because, as they can't help it, there's no offence. Surely the same should apply to narcissists, if they can't help it?

And so, can they help themselves?

This is a tricky one. The answer is both yes and no.

For a start, NPD is *not* a defence in law. It is not insanity. Narcissists are perfectly aware of what they are doing, so yes, they can help it. They just don't see, or *can't* see, why they should do any differently. And that's where the 'no' answer comes in.

It can be interesting to read forums online where those few narcissists who admit their narcissism speak of it. They relate things like how, before they accepted their narcissism, they just didn't understand why other people had a problem with their actions. They thought that they, the other people, were just being over-emotional when they complained, and they were the ones with the problem and should just get over themselves. The narcissists go on to say, however – and this is very telling it seems to me – that when they realise the truth, it doesn't make any difference to them. They now acknowledge intellectually that they hurt and damaged people, but it just doesn't make any difference. That knowledge doesn't impact them in any way. It's just a fact, but not a terribly relevant one. And it definitely doesn't make them change their behaviour.

I only dimly understand how a narcissist thinks, in as much as I think any non-narcissist can understand it. I think of it like this: I jettison yesterday's newspaper without a worry or thought or concern once it stops being of use to me. I don't stop to think what the newspaper thinks of that treatment. Why should I? The newspaper is nothing, it has no needs or wants, and therefore the only thing that matters in the equation is what *I* want; in this case, for the newspaper to be gone out of the sitting room so the room can be tidy.

Narcissists view other people as having as little value, or rights, as a newspaper. They don't articulate this to themselves, of course. They are not introspective at all as already said. But that's what it amounts to.

So, I theoretically *could* treat the newspaper with more respect. I *can* help what I do with it. I just choose not to because it is not necessary to do so.

To my best guess, this is how it is with narcissists.

So, do I need to be forgiven for just jettisoning the newspaper? Does the tornado need to be forgiven for destroying a town? Does the toddler need to be forgiven for drawing on a wall?

In a way they are nonsensical questions, aren't they? There was no crime committed, no matter the damage to the newspaper, the town, the wall. And so forgiveness is a moot point.

Maybe the same applies to narcissists.

So we don't forgive her, but not because we're bearing a grudge, but because it's an irrelevant concept in this case.

We can look at it another way too: The fact is that the word 'forgive' itself is quite a woolly one. It has several meanings.

The first is in the sense of 'to forgive a debt'. Your mother owes you a debt for her ill-treatment of you, no doubt about that. Not necessarily money, but hey, therapy doesn't come cheap. But a debt of acknowledgment for sure, and reparations in whatever way would be possible. But the thing is, she doesn't acknowledge that debt, and has no intention of paying it, and never will. So, for you to forgive that debt is to write it off, so to speak. It is to accept that your mother will never make up to you for what she did – and to let that be okay. To accept it calmly and philosophically. That is not an easy place to get to, but I suggest it is well worth trying as it frees *you*.

The second meaning of 'forgive' is to 'cease to feel resentment towards'. Again, if you can do this, it is hugely empowering for you. Your resentment is a tie between you and her, and cutting that tie will free you. Your resentment is a knot of acid in your own heart, and even your own body, and it does you no good. The more you can forgive her, in this sense, the better for you. No, she does not deserve to be forgiven like this. But this isn't about her, it's about you.

The third meaning, often used, is 'to say it was okay that it happened'. And that is the meaning that DONMs, rightfully, resist. It was *not* okay that it happened. She was totally wrong to do what she did, and nothing will ever change that. You never have to try to persuade yourself otherwise.

Another reason that DONMs resist forgiving their mothers is that they think it means letting her back into their lives. This is categorically not so. You can forgive from a safe distance. Forgiveness absolutely does not mean that you have to subject yourself to more abuse. That was the mistake my mother was making.

Yes, if there were a case where someone did something wrong to you, and they were genuinely remorseful, and apologised, and made suitable reparations, and you knew that they fully intended never to repeat the offence, then forgiveness can, and would, include resuming the relationship. But that does not apply to narcissistic mothers.

And so, in summary, I think that forgiving them in the first and second meanings is good to aspire to, because it heals us and frees us. It's something we do for us, and that can only be good. The third meaning should never apply. And no meaning should mean we have to let her continue to abuse us.

But even for the first and second meanings – I don't necessarily think it should be a goal by itself, because then it can put pressure on us if we don't succeed. I think it is a valid end result of our own healing when we do it, and perhaps how we feel about forgiving her (in that sense), is a good marker of how our healing is going.

Another way to describe forgiveness is this: To give up the wish that things could have been different. In other words, to release any attachment or desire about her being the mother you wanted, or you having the mother you wanted. This might sound very Buddhist, and in a way it is, but just by coincidence. But it is true what they say that the only source of suffering is desire. All suffering is caused by us wanting things to be different than what they are. The more we accept things as they are without resistance, the less we suffer.

10
THERAPY

For years I did not have therapy. This was partly cultural as therapy wasn't common in my time or place. And it was partly that I just thought I was born broken and so I didn't think there was any way to fix me. Also there was an element that I learned early not to rely on others. And as part of doing things myself I did a lot of healing myself with EFT – I do credit EFT with me being as well, as whole and as happy as I am (to the extent that I am well, whole and happy – it's still a journey and a process).

But my colleague Light (she of lightshouse.org fame) persuaded me to try therapy. She said that I would get gifts out of it I had not even expected, and could not imagine.

And so I did, and it was very empowering. The validation was huge, and it is hard to give that to yourself. Also a healthy and objective perspective on myself was a revelation. For example, I remember with shock when my therapist told me I was too hard on myself. I had always thought I was too easy on myself and let myself away with far too much! That was an interesting perspective which has changed how I treat myself massively, and which I would never have experienced otherwise.

But the therapy has to be the right therapy, with the right therapist, and there are a lot of bad ones out there. Light taught me how to shop for a good therapist.

- Don't be scared to shop around. Despite what you think, you do not have to take the first therapist you speak to. Having the right therapist is an extremely important decision and you need to get it right. Speak to them on the phone first. (And if, as happened to me on more than one occasion, they are far too important to speak to you on the phone, move right along.)

- Trust your gut. If you don't like them or don't feel comfortable with them, then don't take it any further. It's the therapist's job to establish rapport and make you feel comfortable, and you should experience that immediately. They should do a good (i.e. feels right to you) mix of allowing you to speak but also of guiding the conversation where you are struggling. Too many I spoke to just went into a long sales-spiel of a speech, with no reference to me. Others said they would answer questions, but when I said I didn't even know what questions to ask, they left me floundering. The wonderful woman I ended up seeing, when I said that, immediately picked up the slack and 'carried me' so to speak, but in a supportive rather than over-bearing way.

- This is essential: Make sure your therapist knows about Narcissistic Personality Disorder. A frightening number of them do not. So as part of your phone interview ask them what they know about NPD, and if they don't answer satisfactorily, move on. We have had cases on the forum of therapists who, clearly not understanding NPD, tried to get the DONM to re-establish contact with her mother, and/or invalidated her experiences.

- Know what their credentials are, and what they mean. Do your research on that.

- Above all do not let them invalidate you, or your experiences, or opinions. You have been brought to therapy by a lifetime of invalidation; you do not need more. This is not to say that they cannot offer you different perspectives – indeed, they need to, to help you move on. But they can do it without invalidating your current perspective. Here is the flavour of feedback you are looking for: 'I can totally see why you would see it that way; it does fit the evidence. But would you consider this alternative interpretation of the evidence?' Not, 'You are wrong to think that'.

- Asking questions has two benefits: not only will give you the answers to the question you ask, but how the therapist reacts to your question will also tell you a *lot*. Don't just listen to the information you're given, listen to *how* it is given. Does the therapist resent you asking this? Is she impatient? Dismissive? Patronising? Any of those things will be red flags. Don't hesitate to move on.

- It may well feel threatening to interview them in effect. This isn't surprising given your upbringing. But try and see it as a new skill, a new way of behaving in the world. You are changing a lot now, and this is one big step.

- Here's another thing – you don't need a reason to move on. You can just do it. You don't have to justify to yourself, or anyone, why you didn't pick a particular therapist. If it doesn't feel right, then move on.

- Think of the relationship as a courtship. Have a few 'dates', i.e. appointments, first, to see if they are right for you, before committing to them.

- To quote Light : *Among other things, the right therapist will make you feel:*
  Validated
  Safe
  Heard

Comfortable
Understood
Connected
Occasionally challenged, but never threatened
Seen for who you are.

Finding the *right* therapist may take a while, but is *very* worth the bit of extra effort. You'll be very glad you chose well.

11
EFT –
EMOTIONAL FREEDOM
TECHNIQUE

I have spent many years looking into ways of healing. Of course, for most of those years, until I had the N-realisation, I thought it was about fixing a broken me rather than healing a wounded me. But no matter. The resources and epiphanies are still good.

The major tool I would like to share is an amazing technique called EFT. EFT stands for *Emotional Freedom Technique*, and that's what it does: It gives emotional freedom. It literally erases all the negative emotions around an event, so that we can remember it with total calm. And more, it's great for erasing the kind of false limiting beliefs that our mothers implanted in us (see more about Beliefs on page 120) the ones which keep us living small, and in so doing allowing new, true, empowering beliefs, or at least, possibilities, to take root.

Note: EFT is very good to use ourselves, and I offer this here. But often there are issues or experiences that are too big for you to deal with by yourself with simple EFT, and so if the EFT does not work for you, then I do recommend that you work with an EFT practitioner. There is a lot more that can be done than I can share here. It's the difference between first aid, which we can do ourselves and which is very effective as far as it goes, and major surgery which is sometimes needed and which takes an expert. Having said that, it is well worth you trying EFT for yourself as it will work for most people most of the time.

Also, EFT is safe and comparatively very gentle, but even so I need to stress that you take responsibility for your use of this process. The process can involve tears and emotional pain, just as the lancing of a boil involves pus and mess. In both cases, the poison existed anyway; it was only exposed by the treatment, and the mess is temporary as, once exposed, it can be easily cleaned up. In EFT terms, 'cleaning up' means erasing that hurt and pain until only peace remains.

EFT involves nothing more than simple tapping on acupuncture points on the face, hands and torso whilst speaking of your issue.

I understand that you might be sceptical; I was too, when I first heard of it. But I do invite you to reserve judgment and try it for yourself before deciding. It is not faith healing; you do not have to believe in it for it to work. You need only try it with an open mind and see what happens. There are many studies too, proving its efficacy. If you do a search for 'EFT research' you will find links to the latest.

EFT INSTRUCTIONS

If the issue is immediate and you are feeling the emotion right now – for example, if you just got off the phone after a frustrating and upsetting conversation with your mother (i.e. a typical conversation!), and you are all wound up – then what you do is to just tap on the points in order. You don't have to say anything – although you can if you feel moved to do so – just tap the points in order over and over. The instructions on how to do this are below, or go to http://daughtersofnarcissisticmothers.com/eft-instructions.html to watch a video on how to do it.

Remember, too, to breathe as you do this – try to breathe from your diaphragm and not from the top of your chest as we're prone to do when stressed. After a few minutes you will find yourself calming, your upset evaporating until your equanimity is restored and you are not bothered any more by the conversation. You might even be mildly amused by it.

> In fact, you can use EFT whenever you are upset about anything. It is an incredible tool. So if you have a near-miss in the car, or are stressed about a forthcoming job interview – use EFT. Also you can use it on children, just tap on *them* on the relevant points, if they're upset.

However, most of the work we will be doing will be on old issues. Memories, events that still hold trauma for us, and so on. In this case we have to identify the issue first. And so, pick an event to work on.

EFT works best with specific events, such as, 'The time my mother slapped me on my 6th birthday', rather than global events such as, 'My mother was always mean to me'. Or rather, it *does* work on the global events, but obviously progress is slow and imperceptible on such a large issue, such that you would give up doing the work long before you saw any benefit. The old phrase about eating an elephant one bite at a time applies here.

This specific event should also still upset you when you think of it. If it doesn't upset you, it doesn't need healing, after all. Give that upset a score, where 0 is 'this event doesn't bother me at all' and 10 is the highest level of upset you can possibly think of.

For the purposes of this exercise pick an event which has a score of at least 8. EFT works on upsets no matter how small, but to practise and test the process, choose one with a high score.

Here are the tapping points. Note that you can tap either side of the body even though the diagram just shows one side.

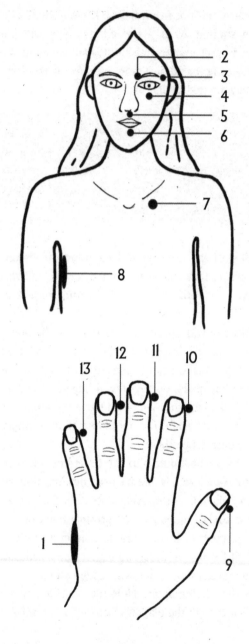

No.	Point Name	Description
1	Karate Chop	The fleshy part of your hand between your little finger and your wrist – where you would hit the wood if you were doing a Karate Chop
2	Eyebrow	In between your eyes at the inner edge of your eyebrow
3	Outer Eye	Where your eyebrow ends
4	Under Eye	The bone just under your eye
5	Under Nose	That little dimple between your nose and top lip
6	Chin	Just under your bottom lip, before your chin itself begins
7	Collarbone	Just under your collarbone
8	Under Arm	Under armpit at about the level of your nipples
9	Thumb	Beside your thumb-nail, the side nearest your body
10	First Finger	Beside your index finger-nail, the side nearest your body
11	Middle Finger	Beside your middle finger-nail, the side nearest your body
12	Ring Finger	Beside your ring finger-nail, on the side nearest your body.
13	Little Finger	Beside your little finger-nail, the side nearest your body.

So, you have picked your issue, and you are referring to the Tapping Diagram.

Next, tap on the Karate Chop point, stating out loud three times (obviously, substitute your own issue for my example): 'Even though she slapped me at my birthday party, I completely love and accept myself.'

I know it might be hard to say you deeply and completely love and accept yourself, but do say it anyway. You don't have to believe it; just say it.

Then tap on each of the remaining points about 7 – 9 times (just guesstimate, don't count, as you want to be thinking about the issue, not about counting), stating just the issue, e.g.: 'She slapped me on my 6th birthday party'.

At its simplest, just keep repeating the issue statement. But it can be helpful to expand on that as new awarenesses come to you, as they will. So you can go into kind of freeform statements: 'She slapped me at my 6th birthday party – that wasn't fair – I didn't deserve that – it ruined the day for me – it was so unfair – how dare she do that – I'm so angry about that.'

Definitely don't fret over this freeform stuff. The EFT process will work just by repeating the issue statement. This is just a suggestion.

Once you have tapped each of the points, that is one complete 'round' of EFT. So do this again, twice, for a total of three rounds.

Now, tune into how upset you are about the issue and see what your score is now. Most likely the upset about the issue will have lessened. Maybe instead of being an 8 as it was when you started, it is now a 7 or even a 6. If this is so, you are on the right track. Do another 3 or 4 rounds, and check your progress. It might be at a score of 3 after that. Simply keep going until your score is a 0.

> It is very possible that as you are tapping on the birthday party issue, other memories will come up. If so, just pause in the tapping to write them down, and then continue with the original issue until it's sorted. You can work on the other issue(s) next.

Another possibility is that your score has actually gone up. This is not a problem at all. It is just that as you tune into the issue you are accessing more of the original upset, which was buried and suppressed. Keep tapping and the score should start to come down.

The other possibility is that no matter how much you tap, the issue will not shift at all. I suggest not tapping any more than 5 rounds – if it has not shifted at all in that time, then you need to look further. There are several things you can try.

The first, and easiest, is to drink some water and make sure you are well-hydrated as that is essential for EFT to work. Also, move around physically a bit, and stretch. Then try again – in a good number of cases that will solve the problem.

If not, there may be something blocking the healing. And so, try doing the script for 'Blocks To Healing' on page 186. Using EFT to help you successfully do EFT might seem counter-intuitive, but that is one of its strengths, that we can use it to use it!

If it still does not work, then it might well be worth getting in touch with a local EFT practitioner as they will have skills to dig out the blocks to healing. In most cases, however, it will not come to that.

Be aware too that you can stop EFT before the issue is completely sorted – if you run out of time for example. Just make sure you don't stop while you are upset in any way – it can be tempting to avoid the pain by suppressing it again and distracting ourselves. Try not to fall into that trap. And don't put yourself through the trauma of leaving yourself upset. But if your score went from an 8 to a 4, and you had to stop then, that's fine. You can pick it up again, still at a 4, the next time.

You can even use EFT to deal with very traumatic stuff. (Although, again, you do this at your own risk. But this process is very gentle and should not cause you any problems.)

The trick with traumatic issues is to work through metaphor, as our subconscious works very well with metaphor.

What you do is this: in your imagination, place the traumatic incident in a sturdy wooden box and cover with a wooden lid. Nail that lid down. Then put that box into another box, this one made of steel. Close the steel lid and lock it with a strong padlock. Then place that steel box into a concrete casing and seal it shut.

Then, look up and you will see that in the far distance there is a mountain. Using the power of magic (or binoculars if you prefer!) you can see the top of that mountain. There is a cave there with a huge stone in front of it. Using more magic, move the concrete case into the cave and roll the big stone over the mouth of the cave.

Now, we work in reverse. Picture the concrete case safe in that cave, and check in with yourself to see how upset you are about it. Do *not* think of the incident in detail, or at all. Think only of the concrete case. Your subconscious knows what it represents. If the score is greater than 0, start tapping using this phrase: 'Even though this concrete case, I deeply and completely love and accept myself."

I know this makes no sense, but it will work. What you are really saying is, 'Even though I have this major trauma represented by this concrete case, I deeply and completely love and accept myself', but the subconscious will be well able to work with the short version.

So, use the EFT process on that phrase, until when you think of the concrete case in the cave, there is a 0 of upset.

Now, consider the prospect of rolling back the stone. Do not actually do that yet. Just consider the idea. How do you feel about that? Does your stress level go up? To what number? With this process, ideally the upset will only go up to a 3 or 4 each time. We are aiming to keep this gentle and un-traumatic. But if it does go up higher than that, reverse the story-line, e.g. stop considering the prospect of rolling the stone back, and go back to tapping on the previous statement about the concrete case for a few minutes, before testing again.

And then, when you have established the score at the prospect of rolling back the stone, use the EFT procedure on the statement, 'Even though it's not safe for me to roll the stone back,

I deeply and completely love and accept myself.'

Continue tapping, using that statement, until you feel total peace, a Level-0 of upset, at the prospect of rolling the stone back. And then, do that very thing – roll the stone back now. But by the power of magic you are still at the bottom of the mountain, far away, and very safe.

So, the stone is rolled back. How do you feel now? There might be a twinge of stress as the concrete case is now more accessible. If so, tap on that: 'Even though the cave is now open, I deeply, etc', and work on that until you are a Level-0 of distress about the concrete case being in the open cave.

Next, consider the prospect of moving the concrete case out of the cave, to just in front of it. And then do the same procedure: if there is distress at that prospect, tap on that statement, i.e. 'I'm scared to move the case out in front of the cave', until the distress is gone. And then move the concrete case out of the cave and place it just in front of the cave.

Little by little you will do the following, tapping to a 0 at each step:

- Consider the possibility of bringing the concrete case down to the foot of the mountain.
- Actually bring the concrete case down to the foot of the mountain.
- Consider the possibility of bringing the concrete case from the foot of the mountain to where you are.
- Actually bring the concrete case from the foot of the mountain to where you are.
- Consider the possibility of jimmying open the lid of the concrete case.
- Do open the concrete case.
- Consider the possibility of taking out the steel case.
- Take out the steel case.

- Consider the possibility of taking the padlock off the steel case.
- Take the padlock off the steel case.
- Consider the possibility of taking the lid off the steel case.
- Take the lid off the steel case.
- Consider the possibility of taking the wooden box out of the steel case.
- Take the wooden box out of the steel case.
- Consider the possibility of taking the nails out of the wooden box's lid.
- Take the nails out of the wooden box's lid.
- Consider the possibility of opening the wooden box.

Once you are at a 0 for the prospect of opening the wooden box and looking at the issue itself, then you can do that. Take it out, and see how you feel. You should find that any upset or trauma is minimal. All the time you have been tapping on the issue of caves and boxes, you have really been healing the trauma of the incident, using the power of metaphor.

Maybe the issue is now only at a Level-2 or Level-3 of upset now. And so, tap using the statement of the actual issue, and erase it totally.

The whole baby-steps thing might seem a bit of a procedure, but compare how long traditional therapy would take to do the same job. With EFT it should take no more than a couple of hours. And that time can, of course, be broken up into different sessions; it doesn't have to be all done at the same time.

PERSONAL PEACE PROCEDURE

This is a very empowering exercise. What you do is to take a sheet and write out every upsetting incident in your life to date, and allocate a score to each one. Then, over a few months, use EFT to erase one or two a day. This means that over time you will be carrying no trauma at all from your past.

EFT FOR LIMITING BELIEFS

Refer to the information about beliefs on page 120.

Once you identify your belief, use that as your tapping statement. So, e.g., 'I'll never amount to anything'.

Or, if you don't know what the belief is, just tap for the issue that's blocking you, e.g., 'I can't make myself phone the prospective clients'. By doing that, the belief underneath that blockage will come to your awareness very quickly, such as the fact you'll never amount to anything so there's no point even trying.

Just keep tapping, observing what happens for you. There will be probably a fairly quickly moving variety of experiences.

When you start the tapping then it'll feel very true and very right to say the statement: 'I'll never amount to anything'. It sits right. It belongs. You might find yourself nodding your head in agreement, even.

But emotions might come up even so. You might, for example, feel very sad. It is sad, after all, to 'know' that you'll never amount to anything. So you can change your tapping statement to, 'I'll never amount to anything and I feel very sad about that'. But you don't even need to do that, you can keep to the original statement and just feel the sadness. It's important though that you allow the sadness to *be*. Don't, if at all possible, run from it or hide from it. It will hurt, yes, but it will be bearable. You may cry. That's okay. Just allow it to *be*, and feel it. Your narcissistic mother no doubt never allowed you to feel your authentic emotions and it's part of your healing journey that you reverse that, and that you *do* feel your authentic emotions.

And, while you're feeling your emotions, keep tapping. Above all, keep tapping, that's essential. It's the tapping that will process and release the sadness (or other emotions that may come up) rather than having them just brought up and hanging around, upsetting you.

And then, after a while the statement, 'I'll never amount to anything' might feel a bit less true. A bit strange even. It's as if, when you started tapping that statement felt very hard, and solid, and concrete. And now it feels a bit softer, a bit less definite.

A new, different truth might zip into your awareness, and out again, too fast for you to identify it, like something spotted out of the corner of your eye.

Just keep tapping, it'll come back and stay longer each time, and eventually you'll be able to focus on it, and realise that it's a new, more empowering, truth. Such as, 'I might amount to something. The game isn't over yet. I've already amounted to lots of things', etc etc.

Tapping affirmation

One very powerful affirmation is this:

I am not who she said I was.

That's it. Just seven words. But they encompass so much about our situation. We have this whole self-image that she created. The horrible-you mirror and so on. And it's not true. So by tapping while you say this statement, you are handing back to her all her false statements about you, and leaving space to find out who you really are.

So, tap on the EFT points while saying this statement, once per point, as often as you can. Try to weave it into your day so that it becomes habit – while you're on the toilet, maybe. Just after brushing your teeth. When you come in the door. The more you do it, the more you free yourself from the toxic web she wove for you, of her beliefs about you.

You can vary it, if you like, to say, 'I am not who you said I was', and imagine yourself saying it to her directly.

This affirmation, combined with the tapping, is extremely powerful, no matter that it looks so simple.

EFT for addictions

We spoke earlier of how DONMs can be at risk for addictions. EFT is very good for erasing these addictions. I used it myself to *finally* give up cigarettes after nearly 20 years' on-and-off addiction. Using EFT for clearing addictions can require dedication though, and commitment. You can approach the addiction from three different angles:

- Every time you get a craving for your addictive substance, tap on that issue, e.g. 'This need for a cigarette'. This should help the immediate craving pass, but will not solve the addiction itself. One challenge is to actually do this. I remember when I was still addicted to cigarettes, knowing I could tap away the craving, thinking, 'I don't want to *not want* the cigarette; I want to *have* the cigarette'. But if you can bring yourself to tap for the craving, it works well.
- Think how you feel about the prospect of never having your addictive substance again. Then, tap on what arises. The panic, the fear, the devastation. You'll probably have to keep doing this over a period of time. That's okay. The addiction is strong and it will not be defeated in one go.
- Think of the benefits the addiction brings you. And don't say that it doesn't bring you any benefits. It does, or you would not do it. If necessary do freewriting (see page 133 for info on that) to see what you get out of this addiction. The way to do that is to have a dialogue between you and your addiction. Start off by writing, 'Hello, Cigarette, I just want to say to you that …' and then freewrite what comes next. And by all means write a letter from your addictive substance to yourself. You will be amazed at the awareness and realisation that comes to you from doing this exercise. And then tap, in turn, for each of those benefits. So, for example, when I smoked I was aware that cigarettes were a friend, that I was never alone once I had a cigarette, that they helped me

cope with crises, that they punctuated the day, that they gave me the excuse to take a break. And then tap for each of those 'benefits' until your cognition changes and you realise it's not a benefit at all, and/or you can get the same benefit (e.g. a break) without a cigarette.

12
EFT SCRIPTS

Here's how it works with these EFT Scripts. They are designed for you to be able to tap away the specific issues, without having to think of what to say. All you have to do is to tap where instructed, and follow the script, preferably aloud. If you spend 10-15 minutes a day, you should find that each issue disappears gradually over 4 or 5 days. You can of course do the tapping in one block, until the issue is gone, but I know from my experience that it's easy to sabotage ourselves when we try to take on too much. Far better to have consistent small amounts.

You might note a difference between these scripts and the EFT instructions. The EFT instructions say to tap the same phrase on each point, but these scripts have different phrasing. That's because the EFT instructions are EFT 101, so to speak. The simplest version. So there is no contradiction.

The scripts that are included are:
1. Tap Away your Self-Care Deficit (page 158)
2. Tap Away the Hope She'll Change (page 163)
3. Tap Away your Grief And Bereavement (page 167)
4. Tap Away the Hurt she Dropped you So Easily (page 170)
5. Tap Away the Fear of Her (page 174)
6. Tap Away your Guilt at Going LC or NC (page 179)
7. Tap Away the Fear of Being Wrong (page 182)
8. Tap Away the Blocks to Healing (page 186)

TAP AWAY YOUR SELF-CARE DEFICIT

Karate Chop	Even though I really struggle with self care ... I love and accept myself anyway. Even though it's such a chore to look after myself and at some level I don't think I'm worth it ... I love and accept myself anyway. Even though I struggle so much with self care ... I love and accept myself anyway.
Inner Eye	I really struggle with self-care.
Outer Eye	I keep sabotaging my attempts to look after myself properly.
Under Eye	I'm just not worth being looked after.
Nose	That's what my mother taught me ... and I learned that lesson well.
Chin	I internalised that lesson very well.
Collarbone	Yes, rationally I know I am worth looking after ... but deep down it does not feel like that.
Underarm	I struggle so much with self care.
Thumb	I really struggle to look after myself.
Index Finger	I always put myself and my needs last.
Middle Finger	It's such an effort to do the things that are good for me.
Ring Finger	I struggle so much with self care.
Little Finger	I'm always sabotaging my own self care.

EFT SCRIPTS

Karate Chop	Even though it's so difficult to nurture myself ... and look after my self-care needs, I'd like to let it be easier. Even though I find it so difficult to nurture myself ... and to look after my needs, and my self-care, I would like to know that it's okay to do that. Even though part of me feels I don't deserve to be nurtured, I'd like to let that belief go.
Inner Eye	It's so difficult to nurture and care for myself.
Outer Eye	It takes so much effort.
Under Eye	I can do it as an effort of will ... but it exhausts me so much ... that eventually I have to stop.
Nose	It exhausts me so much to nurture myself ... and meet my self-care needs ... that eventually I stop.
Chin	It's so difficult to nurture myself ... I don't deserve to be nurtured. ... Rationally I know that's not so ... but that's what it feels like.
Collarbone	My mother taught me that I do not deserve to be nurtured ... and I learned that lesson well ... and I learned that lesson deeply ... and I am still playing that role since then.
Underarm	The truth is that when she didn't nurture me, or meet my needs, it was because of a failing in her. I was only a little girl. I didn't know that. I thought it was my fault. I came to the conclusion that I don't deserve nurturing, and I have believed that ever since.
Thumb	I am carrying the belief that I don't deserve to be nurtured.
Index Finger	I am carrying the belief that I don't deserve to be looked after.
Middle Finger	I am carrying the belief that my self-care needs are unimportant.
Ring Finger	I am carrying the belief that it's not right to nurture myself ... that it's not worth it ... that I am not worth it.
Little Finger	I am carrying the belief ... ever since I was a child ... ever since I was a little girl ... that it's not right to nurture myself.

Karate Chop	Even though I learned as a girl that I did not deserve to be looked after, or nurtured, or minded, I choose to know now that that is a false belief. I came to the wrong conclusion and I have believed it ever since, but it was the wrong conclusion. I saw the evidence of my mother's neglect, and I thought it was a flaw in me, but it was a flaw in her, and I know that rationally now, and I choose to know it in my body as well, and in my subconscious, I choose to relearn the truth.
Inner Eye	I now release this belief that I don't deserve to be looked after.
Outer Eye	I now delete it and erase it.
Under Eye	It's not true, and it doesn't serve me, so why carry it any more?
Nose	I am carrying a little girl's mistake ever since I made it.
Chin	It was reasonable of that little girl to come to that wrong conclusion, but it was still a wrong conclusion, and I don't want to carry it any more.
Collarbone	I am asking my subconscious now, to delete and erase the belief that I don't deserve nurturing or looking after.
Underarm	I am asking my subconscious now to let that belief go. It's not a true belief.
Thumb	I am releasing the belief that I don't deserve to be nurtured or looked after.
Index Finger	I am releasing that belief now. It's not true and it doesn't serve me.
Middle Finger	I am letting that belief go now.
Ring Finger	Deleting and erasing that belief.
Little Finger	Letting it go – letting it all go now.
Karate Chop	I am letting every last bit of that belief go now.

Karate Chop	Even though I had been carrying the belief ... that I don't deserve to be nurtured or looked after ... I choose to let that belief go now ... and I am installing the belief that I DO deserve .... to be nurtured and looked after. Even though I was carrying this false belief ... I am letting it all go now ... I am deleting and erasing it ... and I am choosing to know that I DO deserve to be nurtured and looked after ... and that my self-care needs ARE important ... and that it's okay to look after myself.
Inner Eye	I am now installing the belief ... that it's okay to look after myself.
Outer Eye	That it's more than okay to nurture myself.
Under Eye	That I do deserve to be looked after.
Nose	That I do deserve that my needs are met.
Chin	That I do deserve ... to find it easy ... to look after my self-care needs.
Collarbone	That I DO deserve to be looked after ... and nurtured ... especially by me.
Underarm	I'm installing that belief now ... in my body ... and my subconscious.
Thumb	I am installing the belief that I DO deserve to be nurtured.
Index Finger	And I DO deserve to be looked after.
Middle Finger	And I DO deserve to have my self-care needs met.
Ring Finger	I do deserve to be looked after.
Little Finger	I do deserve to be nurtured.
Karate Chop	I do deserve to have my self-care needs met.

Karate Chop	I choose to find it very easy to meet my self-care needs.
Inner Eye	I choose to be amazed and delighted ... at how easy I find it ... to meet my self-care needs.
Outer Eye	I choose to find it very easy ... and effortless even ... to meet my self-care needs.
Under Eye	I choose to be amazed and delighted ... how easy it is to meet my self-care needs.
Nose	I choose to experience ... that every day ... it is easier and easier ... to meet my self-care needs.
Chin	I choose to find ... that it becomes more and more effortless ... to meet my self-care needs.
Collarbone	I choose to find that every day ... it is easier ... for me to meet my self-care needs ... and to nurture myself ... and to look after myself ...
Underarm	I choose to find that I even enjoy meeting my self-care needs ... and nurturing myself.
Thumb	I choose to find it easy ... effortless ... and enjoyable ... to meet my self-care needs.
Index Finger	I choose to find that it is easy ... effortless ... and enjoyable to meet my self-care needs.
Middle Finger	I choose to find that it is easy ... enjoyable ... and effortless to meet my self-care needs.
Ring Finger	I choose to find that it is easy ... effortless ... and enjoyable ... to meet my self-care needs.
Little Finger	I choose to be amazed and delighted ... how in every day ... it gets easier and easier ... and more and more effortless ... to nurture myself ... and look after myself ... and meet my self-care needs.

TAP AWAY THE USELESS HOPE SHE'LL CHANGE

Karate Chop	Even though I know that this hope that my mother will love me, and be the kind, loving, interested, nurturing mother that I so want, need, and deserve ... even though that hope is a vain one, and I know it's a vain one, it's too hard to let it go. The alternative is accepting that I will never, ever have a mother, and that's too hard for me to face. Even though I just cannot let go of this hope – no matter that I know it would free me – I love and accept myself anyway. Even though I keep clinging to this hope, despite everything, despite all the evidence, and I know it's not doing me any favours, I love and accept myself anyway.
Inner Eye	I'm clinging to this hope.
Outer Eye	I can't let go the hope she'll change ...
Under Eye	...because what will I be left with then?
Nose	I'll be left with no mother.
Chin	And I know that's what I have now, even with the hope ...
Collarbone	... but I'll have to face the fact that I never will have a mother.
Underarm	I don't want to let go of the hope. It means giving up. I'm not ready to do that, even though I know it would free me.
Thumb	I keep clinging to this hope.
Index Finger	I cannot let go of the hope. .
Middle Finger	I need the hope ... even though I know it costs me so much.
Ring Finger	I need the hope ... even though it keeps be banging against a locked door ... crying to be let in. Maybe the door will open sometime if I bang long enough, or loud enough.
Little Finger	I cannot let go of this hope. It means accepting that I will never have a mother

Karate Chop	Even though I need to cling to this hope, I love and accept myself anyway. Even though I'm clinging to the hope, but I know there's no hope really, I love and accept myself anyway. Even though I keep clinging to this hope, despite all the evidence, hoping that she will become the loving mother I need, I love and accept myself anyway.
Inner Eye	I have to cling to the hope.
Outer Eye	I need to keep hoping.
Under Eye	I cannot give up.
Nose	Some day I might find the magic words, or the right phrase, or the right level of passion, or whatever it takes, to get through to her.
Chin	Some day it might all work out, if I keep trying. If I give up hope, it'll never work out. I'll never have the mother I need, want and deserve.
Collarbone	Rationally I know that I will never have that mother anyway, whether I keep hoping or not. She is not capable of being that mother.
Underarm	All the hope does is to keep me trapped.
Thumb	It keeps me banging against a locked door.
Index Finger	Or like a bird constantly banging against a window, trying to get out.
Middle Finger	What I tried before did not work. But if I try it harder, or again, this time it might work. That is the hope.
Ring Finger	But no matter how hard, or consistently, that bird bangs against the window, it will never open.
Little Finger	The only source of freedom for that bird is to find another way out, to look for the open window or the open doorway.

Karate Chop	And maybe that applies to me too. I'm looking for love from my mother in order to be happy, but maybe I need to find my happiness somewhere else.
Inner Eye	By constantly going to an empty well, I'm using a lot of energy and focus, and time, that could be spent looking for happiness elsewhere.
Outer Eye	Even, looking for happiness within. Maybe I could be my own mother.
Under Eye	Maybe I could let go of this hope now. It really is not serving me.
Nose	I would like to be free. Free of the treadmill of looking for her approval and her love and her respect and her kindness.
Chin	But I know those things don't even exist. She cannot give me what she does not have.
Collarbone	So maybe I could let go of the hope. It is not doing me any favours. It is trapping me.
Underarm	Maybe I could accept the truth, and the truth will set me free, like a bird who has finally found the open window.
Thumb	Maybe I could let go of the hope. It is a false hope. It is a useless hope. It is trapping me.
Index Finger	Maybe I could accept that she will never be the mother I need, she will never be the mother I want. She will never, ever, be the mother I deserve.
Middle Finger	I can wish that weren't so. I do wish it weren't so. But it is reality.
Ring Finger	And there is no point arguing with reality.
Little Finger	Maybe I could give up the hope, and the truth shall set me free.

Take a deep breath here. And as you exhale, visualise the stale useless hope flooding out of you as you breathe out

Karate Chop	Even though I'm still carrying this hope, I'd like to let it go now. It does not serve me. It is not my friend. Even though I'm still carrying this left-over hope – I've done it for so long, it feels comfortable. It will feel strange without the hope. But I'd like to let it go anyway. I'll get used to being without it and it will be fun and exciting to explore all the different ways I can be without being trapped in this false hope. Even though I am still holding onto this hope, I'm choosing to let it go now – it is not my friend, it is keeping me trapped. I will be far better off without it.
Inner Eye	Releasing this hope now.
Outer Eye	Letting the hope go now.
Under Eye	Letting that old, stale, putrid, gone-off hope go now.
Nose	Freeing myself from that false hope.
Chin	Freeing myself from this hope that will never come true.
Collarbone	Choosing to accept the reality that she will never be the mother I want, need, and deserve. Yes, that hurts. But banging against that window, banging against that locked door, has hurt so much too.
Underarm	Releasing all this false hope. .
Thumb	Choosing to accept the truth.
Index Finger	Choosing to stop fighting the truth – that's a battle I can never win, and takes so much energy away from what I could be doing.
Middle Finger	Choosing to release the hope and accept the truth that she will never be the mother that I want, need, and deserve.
Ring Finger	Choosing to accept the sadness of that but to see also the freedom and the peace.
Little Finger	Choosing to accept the truth that she will never change.
Karate Chop	Choosing to feel serene and calm as well as sad about the truth, but choosing to feel excited about the freedom it will give me.

TAP AWAY YOUR GRIEF AND BEREAVEMENT

Note: As you're tapping for this, you'll see that I say 'mother/parents' – you need just say whichever of those applies to you.

Karate Chop	Even though I'm feeling such grief at the loss of my mother/parents, I love and accept myself anyway. Even though there's such pain and hurt and loss now that I've lost my family, I love and accept myself anyway. Even though I'm grieving the mother/parents I should have had, as well as the loss of the ones I did have, I love and accept myself anyway.
Inner Eye	This hurt.
Outer Eye	This loss.
Under Eye	This grief.
Nose	It hurts so much.
Chin	It's worse because it's such a private grief.
Collarbone	There's no funeral, no closure, no sympathy from others.
Underarm	But it's no less a grief, and I'm hurting now.
Thumb	This hurt.
Index Finger	This pain.
Middle Finger	This grief.
Ring Finger	The pain of the loss of the mother/parents I should have had, and the letting go of my hope of her/them ever being nice.
Little Finger	This pain and hurt and loss and grief.

Karate Chop	Even though I'm feeling such grief at the loss of my mother / parents, I love and accept myself anyway. Even though there's such pain and hurt and loss now that I've lost my mother and my family, I love and accept myself anyway. Even though I'm grieving the mother / parents I should have had, as well as the loss of the one(s) I did have, I love and accept myself anyway.
Inner Eye	I'm feeling such pain, I can feel it in my body.
Outer Eye	The pain and hurt and loss and grief that I'm feeling.
Under Eye	This pain and hurt and loss and grief.
Nose	I've lost my mother / parents, and it hurts so much.
Chin	This grief and bereavement.
Collarbone	It hurts so much.
Underarm	The loss of the mother / parents I should have had, and the loss of the one(s) I do have.
Thumb	I'm feeling such pain, I can feel it in my body.
Index Finger	The pain and hurt and loss and grief that I'm feeling.
Middle Finger	This pain and hurt and loss and grief.
Ring Finger	I've lost my mother / parents, and it hurts so much.
Little Finger	This grief and bereavement.
Karate Chop	It hurts so much: The loss of the mother / parents I should have had, and the loss of the one(s) I do have.

Karate Chop	Even though it hurts so much, I'm choosing to let the grief go now. Even though there's so much pain and hurt and grief, I'm choosing to process and release that grief now. Even though it hurts so much, I'm choosing to process and release that grief now.
Inner Eye	I'm choosing to let the grief go now.
Outer Eye	I'm choosing to process and release the grief now.
Under Eye	I'm choosing to feel peace and acceptance about the loss of my mother / parents.
Nose	I'm choosing to let the grief go now.
Chin	I'm choosing to process and release the grief now.
Collarbone	I'm choosing to feel peace and acceptance about the loss of my mother / parents.
Underarm	I'm choosing to let the grief go now.
Thumb	I'm choosing to process and release the grief now.
Index Finger	I'm choosing to feel peace and acceptance about the loss of my mother / parents.
Middle Finger	I'm choosing to let the grief go now.
Ring Finger	I'm choosing to process and release the grief now.
Little Finger	I'm choosing to feel peace and acceptance about the loss of my mother / parents.

TAP AWAY THE HURT SHE DROPPED YOU SO EASILY

Karate Chop	Even though I am so hurt that she let me go so easily, I love and accept myself anyway. Even though it hurts so incredibly badly that she just dropped me so easily, I love and accept myself anyway. Even though it hurts and I can feel the hurt in my body, at how easily she let me go, I love and accept myself anyway.
Inner Eye	It hurts so much that she let me go so easily.
Outer Eye	She never made any attempt to fix the situation.
Under Eye	She just let me go. She didn't care.
Nose	And that hurts so incredibly much.
Chin	The pain of this rejection is so deep.
Collarbone	It hurts so much.
Underarm	She just did not care about me.
Thumb	She let me go so incredibly easily.
Index Finger	Just dropped me like yesterday's newspaper.
Middle Finger	I mean nothing to her.
Ring Finger	And that hurts so incredibly much.
Little Finger	The pain of her letting me go so easily.

Karate Chop	Even though her rejection hurts me so much, I love and accept myself totally. Even though her complete indifference towards me hurts me so much, with a physical pain, I love and accept myself anyway. Even though I feel punched in the stomach to have the proof of how little I meant to her, and it hurts so, so much, I love and accept myself anyway.
Inner Eye	It hurts so, so much.
Outer Eye	It's like being kicked in the stomach.
Under Eye	It hurts so much.
Nose	The pain of this hurt.
Chin	The pain of this hurt.
Collarbone	It hurts so much.
Underarm	I can feel the pain in my body.
Thumb	The rejection hurts so much.
Index Finger	She doesn't care about me. She never did. And that hurts so much.
Middle Finger	I can no longer fool myself that she loves me. She does not, and that hurts so much.
Ring Finger	This pain of rejection.
Little Finger	The pain of her indifference.

Karate Chop	It hurts so much.
Inner Eye	I can feel the pain of this rejection.
Outer Eye	The pain of her rejection.
Under Eye	It hurts so much.
Nose	This pain.
Chin	This horrible pain of rejection.
Collarbone	It just hurts so much.
Underarm	The pain of her rejection.
Thumb	The pain of how little I matter to her, or ever mattered to her.
Index Finger	It hurts so much.
Middle Finger	It hurts me so incredibly much.
Ring Finger	The pain of her rejection.
Little Finger	The pain of the proof that I didn't matter to her at all.

Karate Chop	Even though it hurts so much that she thinks so little of me, I'd like to release this pain now. Even though it hurts so much, I'd like to let the pain go. Even though her rejection hurts me so much, I would like to let the pain go, and accept this reality without it hurting.
Inner Eye	I'm now releasing this pain.
Outer Eye	I'm choosing to release the pain of her rejection.
Under Eye	I'm now releasing the pain of her indifference.
Nose	I'm now letting go all of the pain of her rejection.
Chin	I'm releasing all the pain, letting it go.
Collarbone	I'm choosing now to let that pain leave my body, I'm letting it go.
Underarm	I'm choosing to be peaceful about this issue.
Thumb	I'll never be happy about it, but I'm choosing to be peaceful and pain-free about it.
Index Finger	It is what it is.
Middle Finger	I'm releasing the pain.
Ring Finger	I'm releasing all the pain of her rejection now.
Little Finger	I'm releasing every bit of the pain of her rejection now.
Karate Chop	I'm choosing to feel calm and centred about this situation. I'm choosing to feel peace about this situation.

TAP AWAY THE FEAR OF HER

Karate Chop	Even though I'm so scared of her, I love and accept myself totally. Even though I'm petrified of her rages, I love and accept myself totally. Even though I'm so scared of her and her rages, and her temper, and they make me feel like a little helpless girl all over again, I love and accept myself anyway.
Inner Eye	I'm terrified of her rages.
Outer Eye	I'm terrified of her temper.
Under Eye	I'm terrified of her anger.
Nose	I'm terrified of what she might say ... what she *will* say if I stand up to her.
Chin	I'm terrified of her.
Collarbone	I switch back into being a little girl, a little powerless helpless girl, when she starts these rages.
Underarm	I'm terrified of her.
Thumb	I know I'm a grown woman, but when she goes into her rages, I'm right back to being a helpless little girl.
Index Finger	Her rages overwhelm me. They terrify me. I have no power against them.
Middle Finger	I am so scared of her and her temper, and her anger. Even a cross word, or a bitter look ... I am terrified of her.
Ring Finger	I am so scared of her.
Little Finger	I am so scared of her.

If possible, tune in now into your body and feel the fear. Think of her being angry at you or shouting at you, or whatever way it usually manifests, and just be aware of the fear and the panic, and the flight–or–fright experience in your body. Observe those feelings, not running from them, but not drowning in them either.

If you can't feel anything in your body at the thought of provoking her anger, that's okay, just tap along anyway. It will still work for you.

Karate Chop	I can feel the fear in my body, sitting there.
Inner Eye	I can feel the fear in my body.
Outer Eye	I can feel it sitting there.
Under Eye	That terror.
Nose	The panic.
Chin	The flight or fright or fight.
Collarbone	I can feel that fear even at the thought of her anger.
Underarm	I am so scared of her.
Thumb	I can feel that fear now.
Index Finger	I feel that fear.
Middle Finger	I feel the fear in my body.
Ring Finger	I can feel the fear in my body at even the thought of her being angry with me.
Little Finger	I can feel that fear in my body.

Karate Chop	This fear.
Inner Eye	This terror.
Outer Eye	The fear of what she might say.
Under Eye	The fear of how she would abuse me ... shout at me ... and say horrible nasty things to me.
Nose	This terror of her.
Chin	It makes me feel like a little helpless girl.
Collarbone	This terror of her.
Underarm	I can feel the fear in my body.
Thumb	I am so scared of her.
Index Finger	I can feel the panic and the flight-or-fright feeling.
Middle Finger	The panic. The terror that she so effortlessly creates.
Ring Finger	This terror in my body.
Little Finger	This fear of her.

Take a deep breath

Karate Chop	Even though I'm so terrified of her, maybe I don't have to be. Even though I'm so terrified of her and her rages, and her anger, maybe I can let that fear go. Even though I'm still so terrified of her, maybe it doesn't have to be like that. Maybe I could let the fear go.
Inner Eye	Maybe I could realise that she's just like a three-year-old throwing a tantrum.
Outer Eye	Maybe I could see her for what she is – a three-year-old throwing a tantrum.
Under Eye	Maybe I could realise that I'm grown up now, that she does not have any power over me any more.
Nose	Maybe I could see it for what it is – all smoke and mirrors.
Chin	My body is attuned to reacting to her rages, but the days when she could genuinely damage me are gone.
Collarbone	All she has is rage and tantrums and insults.
Underarm	But I choose to see them for what they are – the powerless rantings of a toddler.
Thumb	I choose to release all fear of these rages now – they're actually rather pathetic.
Index Finger	I choose to release all fear of these pathetic rages now.
Middle Finger	I choose to see them for what they really are – a three-year-old throwing a tantrum because she can't have her way.
Ring Finger	These tantrums are all she has left, to try to control me with, and I don't have to be scared of them any more.
Little Finger	I choose to release all fear of these rages now – they're actually rather pathetic.

Karate Chop	I'm releasing all fear of her now.
Inner Eye	I'm telling my brain and my body that it's okay to relax, it's okay to let go of the fear.
Outer Eye	There is nothing she can do to me except these impotent rages.
Under Eye	I choose to see her as the three year old she is emotionally, and know that her rages cannot hurt me.
Nose	I'm releasing and letting go and deleting all remaining fear of her rages and her tantrums.
Chin	I'm choosing to feel uninvolved and peaceful around these tantrums and rages.
Collarbone	They are powerless to hurt me, and I'm telling my body and my brain now that it's okay – there is no danger to me.
Underarm	My body and brain don't have to do the flight-or-fight signals because there is no danger.
Thumb	There are only the powerless, pathetic, impotent rages of a three year old.
Index Finger	I'm releasing all fear from all of my body now. I'm letting go every last bit of fear.
Middle Finger	I'm installing peace and indifference now.
Ring Finger	I choose to observe these tantrums neutrally without them affecting me.
Little Finger	I am releasing every last bit of fear from every bit of my body and brain now.
Karate Chop	I am choosing peace, and indifference now. I'm choosing to be able to observe these tantrums now without drowning in them. I'm choosing to see them as pathetic and silly and even mildly amusing. There is no need for any fear any more.

TAP AWAY YOUR GUILT AT GOING LC OR NC

The script speaks of cutting off contact with her. If you are just going Low Contact and are cutting down contact rather than cutting it off, just say that.

Karate Chop	Even though I feel this guilt at the thought of cutting off contact with her I love and accept myself anyway. Even though I feel so guilty at the prospect of cutting off contact with her I love and accept myself anyway. Even though I feel so incredibly guilty ... at the thought of cutting off contact with her ... I love and accept myself anyway.
Inside Eye	I feel so guilty.
Outside Eye	It's just wrong to cut off contact with my own mother!
Under Eye	The guilt is so hard, so painful
Under Nose	I feel so guilty at the thought of cutting off contact with her.
Chin	I *can't* cut off contact with her. I feel so guilty at the thought of doing it.
Collarbone	It's just wrong. It's just plain wrong.
Under Arm	This guilt is overwhelming.
Thumb	So I'm damned if I do and I'm damned if I don't.
Index Finger	If I stay in touch with her I'm miserable.
Middle Finger	But if I cut off contact with her I'm miserable because I feel so guilty. It's a no-win situation.
Ring Finger	It's even wrong to be doing this tapping. It's wrong to get rid of the guilt.
Little Finger	Because if I let go of the guilt, I'll stop seeing her, and I feel guilty at the thoughts of that.

Karate Chop	Even though I feel so guilty about going No Contact, I love and accept myself anyway. Even though I feel so guilty about going No Contact, I love and accept myself anyway. Even though I feel so guilty about going No Contact, I love and accept myself anyway.
Inner Eye	I need to keep this guilt.
Outer Eye	But I don't want the guilt, because it keeps me trapped in this toxic relationship with her
Under Eye	But I can't let go of the guilt, because then I'll just do what I want to do, which is to stop contacting her.
Nose	This guilt is too much, but I need to hang onto it.
Chin	It doesn't matter how abusive she is ... or how badly she makes me feel ... I still have to keep in touch with her. Those are the rules.
Collarbone	But maybe they don't have to be my rules.
Underarm	Maybe my rules say that there's nothing wrong with protecting yourself from an abuser.
Thumb	Being my mother doesn't give her a licence to abuse me.
Index Finger	Maybe there's nothing wrong with protecting myself from an abuser.
Middle Finger	And therefore nothing to feel guilty about. Because I'm doing nothing wrong.
Ring Finger	Maybe it's okay to let go of the guilt.
Little Finger	Maybe there is no need for any guilt.

Karate Chop	Even though I feel guilty about cutting off contact with my mother, I love and accept myself, and I consider the possibility that maybe there's nothing to feel guilty about. Even though I feel guilty about cutting off contact with my mother, I love and accept myself, and I consider the possibility that maybe there's nothing to feel guilty about. Even though I feel guilty about cutting off contact with my mother, I love and accept myself, and I consider the possibility that maybe there's nothing to feel guilty about.
Inside Eye	She'll be sad and hurt and upset if I cut off contact. I don't want to do that to her.
Outside Eye	But I'm not doing it *to* her. I'm merely protecting myself from an abuser.
Under Eye	Her pain is a Natural Consequence of her bad behaviour all these years.
Under Nose	It is not my responsibility to protect her from consequences.
Chin	It really is not, no matter that she taught me differently.
Collarbone	All my life I've been taught that her needs are more important than mine.
Under Arm	All my life I've been taught that her wants are more important than my needs.
Thumb	But it's not true. My needs and wants are important.
Index Finger	And I need and want to protect myself from an abuser. Which is what she is.
Middle Finger	I do not have to feel guilty for that.
Ring Finger	I choose to release the guilt now.
Little Finger	I choose to release all the guilt now, and know it's okay to protect myself from an abuser.
Karate Chop	I choose to release all the guilt now, and know it's okay to protect myself from an abuser.

TAP AWAY THE FEAR OF BEING WRONG

Karate Chop	Even though I'm scared to be wrong, I love and accept myself very much. Even though it makes me feel sick and threatened and stressed to think of being wrong, I accept that feeling now. Even though I just can't be comfortable with being wrong, I accept myself anyway, and acknowledge that that is just what I was taught.
Inner Eye	It's not safe to be wrong.
Outer Eye	I have to be right, or my whole Self will be annihilated.
Under Eye	It's just not safe to be wrong.
Nose	I have to be right about everything, or I am nothing.
Chin	It's not safe to be wrong.
Collarbone	I feel the tension in my body when I think of being wrong.
Underarm	It's just too scary to be wrong.
Thumb	I can feel the tension in my body when I think of being wrong.
Index Finger	I just can't be wrong, it's not safe to be wrong.
Middle Finger	I have to be right, or un-named terrifying things will happen.
Ring Finger	It's so threatening to me to be wrong.
Little Finger	It's not safe to be wrong.

Karate Chop	Even though it's not safe to be wrong, I accept myself anyway. Even though it's so scary and threatening and intimidating to be wrong, I accept those feelings now. Even though it feels so scary and threatening and intimidating to be wrong, I would like to consider that maybe I can accept those feelings and let them go.
Inner Eye	It's not safe to be wrong.
Outer Eye	It feels too threatening and scary to be ever wrong.
Under Eye	I need to be right to be in any way acceptable.
Nose	If I'm less than perfect, I'm totally wrong.
Chin	It feels too overwhelming to consider I might be wrong.
Collarbone	I just can't feel comfortable with being wrong.
Underarm	It just feels too intimidating to consider being wrong.
Thumb	I have this tension in my body at the thought of being wrong.
Index Finger	It's not safe to be wrong.
Middle Finger	It's just not safe for me to be wrong.
Ring Finger	I feel so ashamed at being wrong.
Little Finger	It's not safe for me to be wrong.

Karate Chop	Even though it doesn't feel safe to be wrong, I'd like to consider the possibility that it *is* safe. Even though I'm scared to be wrong, maybe I could allow myself to be comfortable with it. Even though it's scary and threatening and intimidating to be wrong, maybe I could release and let go those feelings. Even though it's scary to be wrong, maybe I could choose to know it's okay to be wrong, and being wrong is just about new information ... and that's okay.
Inner Eye	I'm telling my body now that it's okay to be wrong.
Outer Eye	Being wrong means nothing about me as a person.
Under Eye	It just means I had wrong, or missing, information.
Nose	Every time I find out I was wrong about something, it's a cause for celebration.
Chin	It means I get a more accurate picture of reality.
Collarbone	It means I can grow and develop as a person.
Underarm	It means I can correct errors.
Thumb	I'd like to be really happy when I discover I'm wrong about something, and feel really comfortable with it.
Index Finger	It is no reflection on me as a person. It just means I had wrong, or missing, information.
Middle Finger	I choose to be totally comfortable with being wrong.
Ring Finger	I choose to know it's perfectly safe to be wrong.
Little Finger	I choose to know being wrong just means I now have more, or better, information.

Karate Chop	I choose to know it's completely safe for me to discover I am wrong. I choose to know it's completely safe for me to discover I am wrong. I choose to know it's completely safe for me to discover I am wrong. I now choose to know, with complete certainty, that it's safe for me to discover I was wrong about something.
Inner Eye	It is no reflection on me as a person. It just means I have new or better information now.
Outer Eye	It's actually safer to discover I was wrong, because then I can correct the error.
Under Eye	I choose to feel joy in being wrong, because each time I discover I'm wrong, is the opportunity for more clarity and a better life.
Nose	Being wrong is simply correcting mistakes. There is nothing to be scared of at all.
Chin	It's like changing out of old dirty clothes into new clean ones. The real me is the person wearing the clothes and is unchanged.
Collarbone	I know my narcissistic mother taught me it wasn't safe to be wrong – but that was wrong information and I know it now.
Underarm	I was wrong about being wrong.
Thumb	Being wrong about being wrong is the first thing I celebrate being wrong about!
Index Finger	It's totally safe to find out I was wrong about something.
Middle Finger	I now choose to know, with complete certainty, that it's safe for me to discover I was wrong about something.
Ring Finger	It is no reflection on me as a person. It just means I have new or better information now.
Little Finger	It's actually safer to discover I was wrong, because then I can correct the error.
Karate Chop	I choose to feel joy in being wrong, because each time I discover I'm wrong, is the opportunity for more clarity and a better life.

TAP AWAY THE BLOCKS TO HEALING

Karate Chop	Even though I have some blocks to healing this issue I love and accept myself anyway. Even though I have some blocks to healing this issue I love and accept myself anyway. Even though I have some blocks to healing this issue I love and accept myself anyway.
Inner Eye	I have some blocks to healing this issue.
Outer Eye	Something is blocking me from healing.
Under Eye	Some part of me feels it's not right to heal.
Nose	Some part of me doesn't want to heal.
Chin	I have blocks to healing this issue.
Collarbone	It's not safe to heal this issue.
Underarm	Part of me believes it's not safe to heal this issue.
Thumb	I have blocks to healing this issue.
Index Finger	Maybe it's not safe to heal the issue.
Middle Finger	Maybe I don't deserve to heal this issue.
Ring Finger	Whatever is going on for me it's causing a block to healing this issue.
Little Finger	I have blocks to healing this issue.

Karate Chop	Even though part of me believes that it's not right to heal this issue, or not safe to heal this issue, or I don't deserve to heal this issue, or some other reason to hang onto this issue, I choose to reassure this part of me now. Even though part of me believes that it's not right to get over this issue, maybe it's not safe to get over the issue, I won't know who I'll be without this issue, or I don't deserve to get over the issue, or it's not safe to get over the issue, or maybe some other block I can't even think of, but I need to hang onto this issue, I choose to reassure this part now that it's okay to let go of the issue. It *is* safe to release the issue. I do deserve to heal the issue. I'll still be me once I've healed the issue. It's okay to release the issue.
Inner Eye	These blocks to releasing the issue.
Outer Eye	It's not safe to release the issue.
Under Eye	I don't deserve to heal from this issue.
Nose	All these blocks to healing from this issue.
Chin	Everything that's stopping me from healing from this issue.
Collarbone	All the blocks that are stopping me from healing.
Underarm	Maybe I don't feel I deserve to heal from this issue. Maybe it doesn't feel safe to heal from this issue. Whatever is going on in my subconscious that stops me healing from this issue.
Thumb	All these blocks to healing the issue.
Index Finger	Part of me needs to hang onto this issue.
Middle Finger	Part of me feels it's not safe to let go of the issue.
Ring Finger	It's not safe to release this issue.
Little Finger	It's just not safe to let go of the issue.

Karate Chop	But I choose to know that it *is* safe to heal the issue.
Inner Eye	It is safe to heal this issue.
Outer Eye	I choose to know that it is completely safe to heal this issue.
Under Eye	I choose to reassure the part of me that it's okay to start healing it now.
Nose	I *do* deserve to heal from this issue.
Chin	It's okay to let this issue go.
Collarbone	It's safe to heal from this issue.
Underarm	I choose to let it be okay to let this issue go now, and to heal from this issue.
Thumb	It *is* safe to heal from the issue.
Index Finger	But maybe it's not.
Middle Finger	I *do* deserve to heal from this issue.
Ring Finger	But maybe I don't.
Little Finger	I want to heal from this issue.
Karate Chop	But maybe I'm scared too.

Take a deep breath here

Karate Chop	Even though part of me is still hanging onto this issue, I choose to know it's okay to let it go now. Even though part of me is hanging onto this issue, and doesn't want to heal it, I choose to reassure this part now that it's okay to let it go. Even though part of me is clinging to this issue, I choose to release it all now. I know I can't imagine what it will be like without the issue, but that's okay too. I am making the decision that it's safe to heal it, and I will enjoy finding out what it's like. I know I will be better off without this issue.
Inner Eye	Choosing to know it's safe to heal the issue.
Outer Eye	Choosing to release all blocks that are getting in the way of healing the issue.
Under Eye	Releasing all the blocks to healing now.
Nose	Letting all those blocks go now.
Chin	Choosing to know it's safe to let go of the issue.
Collarbone	Choosing to heal from the issue now.
Underarm	Choosing to heal all blocks to healing now.
Thumb	Releasing all those blocks to healing.
Index Finger	I am now releasing all the blocks to healing.
Middle Finger	Choosing to know, deep down, in the very core of me, that it's okay to heal now.
Ring Finger	Choosing to let the healing happen now.
Little Finger	Choosing to let the healing happen now.
Karate Chop	Choosing to have the courage to heal now.

And take a deep breath here

Appendix I

THE DSM IV DEFINITION OF NPD

The DSM stands for the Diagnostic and Statistical Manual of Mental Disorders and is published by the American Psychiatric Association. We are currently on Edition IV. They are currently working on Edition V, and at the time of writing it looks as if they are going to change how they identify NPD. So by the time you are reading this, all could have changed. Having said that, what will change will be how the professionals identify NPD. NPD itself won't change, and my working definition on page 17 will still hold.

For now, though, here are the official criteria of NPD. There are 9, and any individual only needs 5 to have a diagnosis of NPD.

The individual:

- Has a grandiose sense of self-importance,
- Is preoccupied with fantasies of unlimited success, power, brilliance, beauty, or ideal love,
- Believes that he or she is 'special' and unique,
- Requires excessive admiration,
- Has a sense of entitlement,
- Is interpersonally exploitative,
- Lacks empathy,
- Is often envious of others or believes others are envious of him or her,
- Shows arrogant, haughty behaviours or attitudes.

Appendix II

OTHER PERSONALITY DISORDERS

There are three personality disorders which are 'cousins' to NPD (officially, these three, and NPD, are known as the Cluster B personality disorders). It is possible that your mother could have some of these as well as there is often overlap. These descriptions are only a summary, for more information check out www.lightshouse.org. These three 'cousins' are:

- Borderline Personality Disorder
- Histrionic Personality Disorder
- Anti-Social Personality Disorder

This link will explain more about personality disorders related to Narcissistic Personality Disorder:

http://www.daughtersofnarcissisticmothers.com/related-personality-disorders.html

And for more information on identifying Narcissistic Personality disorder, go to:

http://www.daughtersofnarcissisticmothers.com/narcissism-definition.html

Now You Are Free to Fly

So, here we are at the end of this journey together. You can fly free now, free from the cage of her brainwashing and her lies. Look at the cover of this book – that's you, that bird flying free.

I am more honoured than I can explain that you have allowed me to be your guide for this time that we have spent together. This stage of the journey might be ending but you are now beginning another wonderful journey – to discovering your true self and to living the life you deserve to live. You are free now. I send you all my best wishes for the rest of your journey. If you think it would be helpful, I invite you to join our forum at www.daughtersofnarcissisticmothers.com/discuss.

I do invite you to remember that you are not broken and in need of fixing, despite what she said. You are wounded and in need of healing, that is all. There is no shame in that. And remember too that you are not crazy. Your perceptions are valid and true. Trust yourself. I know that's a big step, and is a skill you need to learn, but it is a very worthwhile goal. Know too that you are stronger than you yet realise. Your mother tried to make you weak, but while she may have hidden your strength from you, she could not destroy it. Your strength remains to be discovered and used and celebrated.

Again, all the very best on your journey. Welcome to your future.

Danu